THE ORESTEIA / APOLLO & BACCHUS

Also by William Whallon

MONOGRAPHS

*Formula, Character, and Context: Studies in Homeric,
Old English, and Old Testament Poetry*
(Center for Hellenic Studies,
Harvard University Press, 1969)

Problem and Spectacle: Studies in the Oresteia
(Heidelberg: Carl Winter, 1980)

*Inconsistencies: Studies in the New Testament,
the Inferno, Othello, and Beowulf*
(Cambridge: D. S. Brewer, 1983)

POETRY

A Book of Time
(East Lansing: Bennett & Kitchel, 1990)

THE ORESTEIA / APOLLO & BACCHUS

The Oresteia
scenarios of the four plays
including the lost satyr play
adapted from Aeschylus

Apollo & Bacchus
scenarios of *Edipus, The Women of Bacchus,
The Duel,* and *Odu*
adapted from Sophocles, Euripides, and Homer

by
William Whallon

THE OLEANDER PRESS

Cambridge · New York

THE OLEANDER PRESS
17 Stansgate Avenue, Cambridge CB2 2QZ

THE OLEANDER PRESS
80 Eighth Avenue, Suite 303, New York NY 10010

British Library Cataloguing in Publication Data
Whallon, William, 1928–
The Oresteia ; Apollo & Bacchus. — (Oleander language and literature series ; v. 18)
1. Greek drama — Adaptations
I. Title II. Aeschylus. Oresteia III. Sophocles. Oedipus the King IV. Euripides.
Bacchae V. Apollo & Bacchus
882′.01

Library of Congress Cataloging in Publication Data
Whallon, William, 1928–
The Oresteia ; Apollo & Bacchus / adapted by William Whallon. p. cm.
Versions of the Oresteia of Aeschylus (scenarios of the four plays, including the lost
satyr play), Oedipus the King of Sophocles, The Bacchants of Euripides, with adaptations
of the Iliad and Odyssey of Homer.
Contents: The Oresteia of Aeschylus — Apollo & Bacchus : Edipus, The Women of
Bacchus, The Duel, Odu.
1. Greek drama (Tragedy) — Adaptations. 2. Agamemnon (Greek mythology) —
Drama. 3. Orestes (Greek mythology) — Drama. 4. Electra (Greek mythology) —
Drama. 5. Oedipus (Greek mythology) — Drama. 6. Dionysus (Greek deity) — Drama. 7.
Apollo (Greek deity) — Drama. 8. Homer — Adaptations. I. Aeschylus. Oresteia.
English. II. Title. III. Title: Apollo & Bacchus. IV. Title: Apollo and Bacchus.
PS3573.H315074 1997   812′.54 — dc21   96-44037

ISBN 0-906672-58-9 (hbk), ISBN 0-906672-59-7 (pbk)

CONTENTS

The Oresteia

Geometry and Wardrobe, 1–8
Synopsis of the Stagework, 9–16
Text of the Four Plays, 17–29, 29–38, 38–43, 44–53

Apollo & Bacchus

Overview and Synopses, *Edipus*, *The Women*, 54–63
Text of *Edipus*, 64–82; Text of *The Women*, 83–94

Overview and Synopses, *The Duel*, *Odu*, 95–97
Text of *The Duel*, 99–107; Text of *Odu*, 108–115

PREFACE

In fifth-century B.C. Athens, a dramatist would present four plays, to be enacted consecutively. Sometimes — as with *The Oresteia* — they were chapters of the same saga; sometimes they were unrelated to each other. Each play had considerable magnitude; so stamina, or devotion, was needed for watching the entirety. Nowadays, if a Greek play is performed, it will usually be a single one only, seeing that our own stamina and devotion are not so great. The plays offered here are in this respect both ancient and modern. With either set, all four are meant to be performed together (though with *Apollo & Bacchus* three or two or one may be done instead), but the overall length is moderate.

The alternation of ode (in a dancing arena) and episode (upon a stage) has not been kept. Nor have the masks been kept. Nor has the custom that female roles should be acted by males, though in all the plays except *Odu* there is, or may be, some tempering of sexual bipolarity. Again excepting *Odu*, the variation in race, amongst ourselves, may in all the plays be turned to an advantage over antiquity. The speech rhythm throughout is between verse and prose, the stress being mainly on every third syllable. Whatever music is used — such as Bacchic woodwinds and Apolline strings — may emphasize recurrence in the action, but should not be heard above the words, nor be memorable in itself.

The Oresteia

Geometry and Wardrobe

The Oresteia of Aeschylus consisted of four plays: *Agamemnon*, *The Libation Bearers*, *The Furies* (= *The Eumenides*), and *Proteus*. The first three have been adapted, keeping the action, changing the words; the last does not survive except in title (and a couple of lines), and has been made anew. The plays are here spoken of as the 1st, 2nd, 3rd, and 4th; but the action is continuous from one to another, with no change of scene.

The aims were these, in ascending order: (a) to include a 4th play; (b) to fashion the work for our time; (c) to maintain the prominence of the groups; and (d) to highlight the parallelism.

On (a) to include a 4th play: The 4th, like the other three plays, alters elements from *The Odyssey*. As was customary, it has a glimmering of the other three, a whiff of magic, and satyrs. Some of the satyrs, though ithyphallic, may be played by females, as some of the furies may be males. For dramatic balance, the priapism should be underdone, not over- (here is a model, drawn from the Pronomos Vase; a horse's tail might be added, as a damper upon the goat's loins).

On (b) to fashion the work for our time: The audience remembered that Hecabe had suckled Hector, but Eurycleia, Odysseus. Was it then his mother, or a woman in bondage, who had suckled Orestes? Though momentous once, the question would dull the edge of a production today, and has accordingly been omitted. So have the third libation, the spear-prize Chryseis, the offering of Pelops by Tantalus, the emblem of Apollo as a curbstone, Hermes as the conveyor of souls, the olive branch of Orestes as a suppliant, and much besides. What remains, such as the name Clytemestra, becomes familiar; no commentary is needed.

One door closed to the ancients is open to us. Cassandra (and the others played by her actor) may be black against a white cast, or white against a black cast, or Chinese against Indian, or whatever. Ruby Dee was Cassandra against Judith Anderson as Clytemestra, at Ypsilanti.

On (c) to maintain the prominence of the groups: All four groups appear in all four plays, each group having a speaking part in (just) one of them, as shown by the italic type, along a diagonal, in the table below:

	1st play	2nd play	3rd play	4th play
old men	*elders of the kingdom*	elders of the kingdom	elders of the kingdom	followers transmute
women	servants of Clytemestra	*servants of Clytemestra*	attendants of Athene	servants of Helen = wives of followers
furies, satyrs	furies	furies	*furies*	satyrs
armed men	contingent of Agamemnon, guard of Egisthus	followers of Orestes, guard of Egisthus	citizens of the kingdom as escorts	*followers of Menelaus*

The members of a group speak separately, not together. The gestures and movement of a group are distinctive, so that the affinities among the plays will be striking. The groups are of the same size: 12 as originally, or 8 or 6 or 4 (if fewer than 12, then Egisthus, at the end of the 1st play, will not be the 13th child, but simply the last).

The four groups may be multiracial, but need not be; there are reasons why the furies should match Egisthus and Clytemestra, and why the armed men should match the women, the old men, and the satyrs; but the matter is a small one.

On (d) to highlight the parallelism: As with the groups, so with the singles. Each of the three actors appears in all four plays, taking all the roles of a kind (the Cassandra is a female who can be a male — Pylades, Apollo, Proteus — or else a male who can be a female). Three distinctive, resonant voices, even melodious ones, will be heard throughout, speaking with bravura at no greater than a moderate rate. And three distinctive faces will be seen throughout, each one being, from role to role, different and yet the same, as with Alec Guinness in *Kind Hearts and Coronets.* It may be that Agamemnon has a bushy black beard, Egisthus a curly brown one, Orestes a pale yellow one, and Menelaus a red one. Clytemestra wears a chaplet of purple or blue flowers, and so does Helen at first, but Helen's is white at the close (Electra does not wear flowers; nor do the group of women; Cassandra wears a chaplet of yellow flowers). If Clytemestra wears a scimitar emblem upon her bosom, Helen may wear a heart. Cassandra, Pylades, and Apollo wear the same robe, but she holds a wand and wears a veil, whereas Apollo has a bow and arrows (Athene has helmet, shield, and spear). The old men lean on staves throughout; the servant women in the 2nd and 4th plays carry various sizes of pitchers; the armed men have spears. And when the same garments are used again (as shown on the page facing) and there is a sameness in demeanour.

actor	apparel	1st play	2nd play	3rd play	4th play
first actor (male)	grandiose white lion on crimson	Agamemnon Egisthus	Orestes, Egisthus	Orestes	Menelaus
second actor (female)	grandiose see-through purple	Clytemestra	Clytemestra		Helen to begin with
"	simple black		Electra		
"	grandiose see-through white			Athene	Helen at close
third actor (m. or f.)	grandiose orange sun	Cassandra	Pylades	Apollo	
"	grandiose orange bull				Proteus
corpses (mutes)	grandiose solid crimson no lion	Agamemnon Cassandra	Clytemestra Egisthus		
cloth strewn (see first actor)	grandiose white lion on crimson strewn before Agamemnon			strewn before Menelaus	
cloth displayed (see corpses)	grandiose solid crimson no lion		by Orestes at close	robes put on furies	
group of old men	homespun color and quality	elders of the kingdom	elders of the kingdom	elders of the kingdom	followers transformed
group of women	simple white	servants of Clytemestra		attendants of Athene	servants of Helen = wives
"	simple black (see Electra)		servants of Clytemestra		
(m. or f.) group of furies; satyrs	grotesque; ithyphallic	furies	furies	furies	satyrs
group of armed men	simple armour	army of Aga. guard of Eg.	fellows of Or. guard of Eg.	citizens as escorts	followers of Menelaus

The watchman and the servant in the 2nd play, performed by a fourth actor, are dressed alike in homespun, and may be regarded as being the same person.

Besides this sameness, with variation, within the roles of the same actor, there is another sameness with variation. Late in the 1st and 2nd plays, the gate is opened wide (and not shut until just before the end), showing a death tableau. Each time, a figure holding a sword stands by two corpses, and a group (of old men in the 1st play, of women in the 2nd) is in the orchestra. Then cloth is placed at the second tableau just where it had been at the first one — placed by the old men on stage in the 2nd play, who take the posture that the women had taken at the close of the 1st. The visual effect — of sameness, or recurrence — is now the greatest in all drama.

An overview of the cloth strewn: a. what group lays the cloth? b. where does the group come from? c. does the group stay by the cloth? d. when does the group take it up? e. what exit does the group leave by? *1st play:* a. women; b. from the middle door, with Clytemestra; c. no, the women leave (when Clytemestra does, by the women's door, just before Cassandra speaks), but return at the death tableau (streaming from the women's door) and assume an abject posture about the cloth; d. just as Egisthus enters upon the stage with his guard; e. by the women's. *2nd play:* a. old men; b. from those round about, or from the audience; c. yes, with the abject posture of the women in the 1st; d. while the women reply to Orestes, just before the furies appear; e. by the men's. *4th play:* a. women; b. from the middle door, with Helen, as in the 1st; c. yes, with the abject posture of those in the 1st and 2nd; d. as soon as Menelaus has entered the house, with Helen; e. by the women's, as in the 1st, but they straightway appear behind the wide gate.

Other instances of parallelism: the cloth is spread in the same manner in the 1st, 2nd, and 4th plays, and by the same women in the 1st and 4th; Clytemestra or Helen, in the 1st and 4th, stands at the middle door, but not on the cloth, as Agamemnon or Menelaus walks upon it; the cloth is taken into the house (for it belongs to the house) in like manner by the women in the 1st and 4th, and by the old men in the 2nd; Agamemnon in the 1st enters the palace with a characteristic gesture, perhaps a swagger, and so does Egisthus in the 2nd, though Egisthus in the 1st and Menelaus in the 4th do not; Clytemestra in the 2nd, Helen in the 4th, fondles her breast at the middle door; the one enters with Orestes, the other with Menelaus, each time his arm about her; the armed men leave alike twice in the 1st (except that the first time they take the chariot with them) and once in the 2nd; a groan or cry from within is heard in the 1st and 2nd; the old men sit on stones around the rim of the orchestra in the 1st, 3rd, and 4th, and the women may kneel between the stones just before the death tableau is shown in the 2nd; the old men are taken from those round about or from the audience, in the 2nd and 3rd.

Surprises enhancing the parallelism: Cassandra goes into the women's door, in the 1st, but her corpse appears as the wide gate opens. Orestes as a guest had entered by the men's, in the 2nd, but when he appears it is at the middle, the door of the rulers. In the 4th, Helen enters the house by the women's but then appears at the middle, and similarly the women, later, enter by the women's but appear at the wide gate. We thought that Egisthus, in the 2nd, had been told to come alone, but when he comes it is with his guard, and then they leave, so that finally he does enter the house alone.

Words repeated between plays (perhaps with changes
in tempo or other variation): 1st and 2nd plays, the murder
of Agamemnon, chanted by Cassandra and then by Pylades,
*In the labyrinth loose is the bull, broken the stones,
hammer upon them, his death fraught with torment* . . . 1st
and 4th plays, at the cloth strewn, *muscle and bone,
strength in will and desire, Hail sword for my scabbard,
dagger for sheathing, fill me with strength, with your love
and your fibre* . . . *lay out the weaving, his emblem before
him, a thoroughfare fine for a god. Let him ruin the scarlet
and crimson* . . . *Comptroller of gods and of men, creator
despoiler, tread it in triumph, rape the rich threading,
deflower its worth, ravish and ravage. Then bathe away
care, I will robe you in honour, and share in the bloodshed.
Brutal my love for the lion* . . . 2nd and 4th plays,
Clytemestra to Orestes (2nd) = Helen to Menelaus (4th),
with an erotic gesture, inappropriate for 2nd and hence
shocking, appropriate for 4th, *Before you would hurt me,
remember my breast* . . . 2nd and 4th plays, the song or
chant of the women with pitchers (which they do not pour
from, since Electra bids them not to), repeated when the
women flutter about, as Electra goes alone after Egisthus,
and again at the end after Orestes has left pursued (2nd), =
the song of the women (but not Helen) as they pour from
their pitchers into the vat, and then ladle up from the vat
into the pitchers (4th), *Drugs from root and from pith,
drugs that soften and soothe, drugs forgiving the past.
Pods of sarcophagus blooms, transmuting the carrion calyx.
Honey from meadows of witchwood and webworm, Lethe-
bank wort soporific to grudges. Tuft of new fleeces to soak
up the bitters, petals like seashells that hear and forget.*

Parallel visionary effects (not to detract from the death tableaux): Cassandra in the 1st play sees the furies on the roof; Orestes in the 2nd sees them in the courtyard. Cassandra in the 1st and Pylades in the 2nd see the murder of Agamemnon through the symbol of a bull — after the designs of Dalí in Hitchcock's *Spellbound* — and describe it in chant, with the same voice. The guises that Proteus says he can assume, in the 4th, may be shown similarly.

Synopsis of the Stagework

Cassandra, Orestes, Electra, and Pylades are in their middle teens; Agamemnon, Clytemestra, Egisthus, Helen, and Menelaus, in their early thirties (all young but with a clear difference between the two generations). The names are pronounced Cas*san*dra, O*res*teez, E*lec*tra, *Py*ladeez, Aga*mem*non, Clyte*mes*tra, E*jis*thus, Mene*lay*us, *Hel*en, A*pol*lo, A*theen*a, *Pro*tyoose. The house is grand in dimensions. Its broad two-leaved central gate opens inward from top to bottom upon an enclosed unroofed courtyard, near the end of the 1st, 2nd, and 4th plays. At the one side of the house are the quarters of the men; at the other, those of the women: these may, but need not, have projecting wings. There are three doors: the one cut into the gate (so that the door may be opened when the gate remains shut) is here called the middle; the others are to the men's quarters and to the women's; each should admit two persons at a time if there are more than six in a group. Before the house is a level area here called the stage; a few steps below it, or at the same height, is a

large circular area known as the orchestra (which an
audience would sit around in the theatre).   In the midst of
the orchestra is a smouldering sunken altar, and along the
rim of the orchestra are smooth stones for sitting on (12 or 8
or 6 or 4, the number of persons in a group).   There are no
other properties.   At each side of the orchestra, near the
stage, is an entrance from (or exit to) town or country: it is
here called a byway.   Nor is there a glimpse of anything
beyond.

Though the action is continuous, there may be breaks,
upon the screen or in the theatre, after the 1st and 3rd
plays: the four plays would then be three parts, entitled
Agamemnon, Orestes, Menelaus.   Or there may be a single
break, after the 2nd play, when the furies from the
courtyard pursue Orestes along a byway, the wide gate is
shut, and the women from the orchestra, singing, enter
through the door into the women's quarters; after the break,
this scene would be repeated exactly, and followed by what
comes next.   But there is no need for a break.   During film
credits, or before the lights are dimmed in the theatre, there
might be the raising of a maypole to Bacchus (Dionysus).
What happens in the four plays is as follows.

1st: Old men from a byway enter the orchestra; they
tell that Agamemnon has come home (with an exotic young
woman), and speak of the sacrifice years before at his
leaving; by and by they sit on the stones. Clytemestra, with
women who are bearing cloth, enters upon the stage from
the middle door; standing near the door, but not blocking
the entrance, she too speaks of the sacrifice, and then tells
of her liaison with Egisthus.   A chariot with Agamemnon

and Cassandra is drawn by armed men, from a byway, into the orchestra; there may be more armed men alongside. Clytemestra hails Agamemnon and savagely bids her women spread the cloth before him. As Agamemnon walks on the cloth, towards the middle door, the armed men leave with the chariot, along a byway. With some characteristic gesture (later used by Egisthus) he enters the house. Clytemestra speaks to Cassandra, moving towards her, and then enters the house, followed by her women, through the women's door. Furies on the roof appear to Cassandra, and to the audience, but not to the old men. She is appalled by the furies, and then by what she sees, as a visionary, through the wall: the murder of Agamemnon by Clytemestra. The old men, sitting on the stones, cannot fathom her words. More soberly, Cassandra tells that Apollo speaks through her as if he were her lover; these words the old men are unwilling to believe. She enters the house by the women's door. As the old men speak of her with pity, they hear groans from within the house, and wonder what to do. The gate is opened wide (as it will remain until shortly before the end) revealing Clytemestra by the bodies of Agamemnon and Cassandra, within the courtyard, close to the gate. Her women, streaming through the women's door, take an abject position by the cloth that had been strewn. (This is the tableau that will be seen again.) The old men rise from the stones and condemn Clytemestra; she replies, with bravura, from the courtyard, and then the wide gate closes, so that she is seen no longer. The cowering women take up the cloth and enter the women's door with it. Egisthus and the men of his guard enter from a byway;

he tells of Thyestes, and enters by the men's door (his actor returning presently as Orestes); the guard leave along a byway as the army of Agamemnon, with the chariot, had done (the armed men returning presently as the followers of Orestes). The old men speak of Orestes and leave along the same byway as the guard had done.

2nd: Orestes, with Pylades and followers, enters from the other byway. With Pylades, Orestes goes to the altar, which is now the tomb of Agamemnon, and consecrates a lock of his hair; they then step aside. Electra, with women bearing pitchers and singing, all from the women's door, also comes to the tomb. She tells the women not to pour on the grave, but on the walls of the house; for she has recognized the token. Orestes and Electra meet and plan vengeance; the women and then Electra enter the women's door. Orestes calls to the watchman, at the men's door, who answers; and Clytemestra appears at the middle door. Orestes tells of a threesome, himself (false name: Rhadamanthus) devoted to hunting, his friend Pylades serving the Sun, and (this false too) Orestes who idles and who lent him the robe he is wearing. Clytemestra orders that they should be admitted, and returns into the middle door. Pylades and the companions enter by the men's door; after a word to the watchman, Orestes follows them. As he does so, women come from the women's door, and speak fearfully of summoning Egisthus with his guard. Electra follows them out from the women's door, and says she will accompany them, and will tell Egisthus to come alone; she then leaves along a byway by herself. The women flutter about, and sing all or some of their song Drugs, and enter the house by the women's door. Egisthus comes with his

guard from a byway; the guard leave (as in the 1st play);
and he enters by the middle door (with the same gesture as
Agamemnon's). A groan or cry is heard (perhaps as in the
1st, perhaps not). A servant comes from the men's door
and says, 'The master is slain, get the lady out, break down
the door'; he then returns by the men's door. Clytemestra
appears at the women's and asks, 'Why the shout?' Orestes, with Pylades, at the middle door, says that Egisthus
would have her company; she goes to where Orestes is, by
the door. He reveals who he is, and she begs for mercy on
her breast. Orestes asks Pylades what he should do;
Pylades speaks in chant of the murder (as Cassandra had
done), and then inaudibly to Apollo, and enters by the
men's door. Orestes and Clytemestra enter by the middle
door, his arm about her, forcibly. The women come from
the women's door into the orchestra and ask, 'Why the
shout?' as Clytemestra had done, and kneel between the
stones. The gate is opened fully, showing Orestes by the
bodies of Clytemestra and Egisthus (Orestes holds a sword
as Clytemestra had done in the 1st play, and also holds the
robe Agamemnon had been murdered with). Orestes calls
out old men from the citizenry round about, to display the
murder robe; they enter from the byways, spread the cloth,
and take an abject position by it (as the women in the 1st
play had done: this completes the parallelism of the
tableaux). Orestes speaks and the women in the orchestra
reply; the old men take the cloth through the men's door
(as the women in the 1st play had taken it through the
women's); and Orestes justifies his deed. Furies appear
from the courtyard (as they had appeared on the roof in the
1st play), and pursue him along a byway; after they leave

the courtyard, the wide gate is shut. The women in the
orchestra sing (or hum) their song Drugs, and enter by the
women's door, while:

   3rd: Orestes pursued by the furies — along the other
byway than the one he had fled by — comes into the
orchestra, which may be the interior of the temple of
Athene (the locale is obscure); he appeals to her at the
altar, as if he were clutching her emblem. The furies join
hands, dance around him, and chant. Athene enters the
orchestra from a byway, says that she felt his touch, and
commands the furies to break their ring. She takes jurors
from the citizenry round about (much the same action, and
the same group, as when old men are gathered by Orestes
in the 2nd play; but the jurors come into the orchestra,
rather than on stage, and sit on stones as in the 1st play).
Athene acknowledges Apollo, who has just come from a
byway. The furies dispute with him for Orestes, the jurors
voting after each argument (genial face + open hand, or
frown + clenched fists). Athene announces that it is a tie,
Orestes is free. The furies say, 'Naught will thrive'; Athene wins them over with promises of honour. She claps,
silently; the women who are her attendants appear from a
byway, with crimson robes, now the colour of nobility, for
the furies. Again, she claps silently, and armed men appear
at a byway, with torches. And now she forms a procession
— the furies, the old men who had voted, the women her
attendants, and the armed men, besides the goddess herself,
Apollo, and Orestes — towards what will be the shrine of
the furies, who are to be called the Kindly Ones. The
procession leaves solemnly but briskly, with humming.

4th: Proteus, from the other byway, with sacks over his shoulder, lugs a vat to the altar in the orchestra, speaks with mime and dance, and utters an incantation.   Armed men enter from the byway that the procession of the 3rd play had left by, speak of Menelaus and Helen, and ask to taste the broth. Proteus offers the ladle and tells of transformation.   The men sip, enter the house by the men's door, and come out at once by the middle door, into the orchestra, as *old* men, who move totteringly and sit on the stones (as in the 1st play).   Proteus continues with his chant.   The (old) men sip again, enter as before, and come out as before, but now as satyrs, who dance a turn.   Proteus continues. The group sip again and enter as before.   Proteus says that now the kettle is dry.   Helen enters from a byway, with her women, who (as in the 2nd play) are bearing pitchers.   She speaks of the brew of forgetfulness she would prepare, against the anger of Menelaus at her infidelity, and the women empty their pitchers into the vat, and sing their song Drugs, about the ingredients. Helen enters the house by the women's door and, as Proteus stirs, the women fill their pitchers with the mixture, and follow her. Menelaus comes from a byway, minded towards punishing her.   Proteus offers him a sip.   Menelaus takes the sip and heads towards the house.   Helen appears at the middle door with her women, who are bearing cloth (as in the 1st play), and hails Menelaus (as Clytemestra had hailed Agamemnon); she bids them lay the cloth, and they do so (where it was in the 1st and 2nd plays).   Menelaus walks on the cloth, but in resentment.   Helen strokes her breast with the gesture that Clytemestra (same actor) had made in the 2nd, standing by the middle door (where Clytemestra had stood in the 1st and the 2nd). They enter together by the middle door, his arm about her (like Orestes and Clytemestra in the 2nd, except that now the gesture is one of love). The women take the cloth through the women's door (they will soon reappear at the middle door). Proteus stirs and chants; the vat bubbles over, for the first time. The wide gate opens, all are smiles for the first time: men and women reunited, leaving the courtyard and entering the orchestra, dance around Proteus with thanks.

Text of the Four Plays

[A group of old men from a byway enter the orchestra, and speak singly:] Agamemnon has kissed the earth. King of the West and the East. Through winding streets, his chariot, cobble to cobble. Open the shutters and pelt him with pomegranate flowers, buds of a summertime apple, sing his arrival. They murmur a woman exotic is with him, a princess or priestess, wild garb and wild eyes, alloted as booty of war. Clytemestra our queen, will she *not* bear resentment, *not* devise malice? Can a wife welcome husband from war, when her rival is with him? Where was his mind when he planned it?

The altar ablaze for thanksgiving, the altar stones wet with libation. Oil of the olive, wine of the grape. Lambs and kids for the roasting: savour the smoke on your lips. May the heavens breathe gratefully, glad of the homage we burn. Thanks for the enemy ruined: the men and boys dead; the women and girls, allotted for whoredom, bartered as drudges, the city walls broken, the ground strewn with salt, that grain cannot grow. A state no more heeded, its annals complete. How happy our mouth as we taste their affliction.

And yet the flame sputters, tears dampen the coals. Where is our own, our army returning, where the great fleet? The countless a handful. Bronze tearing sinew, storm drowning timber. Empty our triumph, barren of joy: sorrow at bedtime, sorrow at rising. Mothers and brides, tending their anguish, begrudging the splendour, hatefully welcome the monarch who trembled the plain.

It is like as it was, years to the hour, time turning like
wheels. Gold and black fires, flocks butchered and burnt.
Flesh to buy favour, offered in homage. So is it now, so
was it then, years to the hour. Flesh to buy favour. It
bought desolation. The bribe was resented. Or else it was
meagre. The winds were adverse, the ships that would sail,
oak of the hillside, ash of the meadow, crashed at the
harbour, tore open and drank. What word from the
prophet, what cost is exacted? What fee for the crossing,
toll at the border? A child was the war-price. The king
gave his first-born, a daughter belovèd, her beauty and
body intact. Then all sobbed aloud. Men smote their
heads with their hands, women tore cheeks with their nails.
[The old men now sit upon the stones.]

*[Entering upon the stage from the middle door, Clytemestra
appears with her women, who are bearing cloth, and
speaks:]* Where is the treasure to pay for my first-born?
What ruby or pearl from the caves of the ocean, gold
outweighing the body, the yield of my womb? Would a
kingdom of fabulous wealth have the worth of the girl that
I bore him? Would the moan of a crucified empire pay for a
note of her voice? What coin for the fruit of my womb,
what coin was it sold for, the womb he maligned?

The womb he left empty, the loins he left lonely, red
ants of desire, crawling and stinging. Whose plough for the
furrow? A field must have tillage, not languish neglected.
Where else the same contour, implement implement, one
for another? The plough of Egisthus, it brings me to
harvest. Same contour, same moulding, the king and his
cousin, same engine and force. Agamemnon Egisthus, ruler

and regent, lion for lion, rampant or couchant. Thighs of like posture, loins of like measure, no telling between them, how *was* I unfaithful? alike as two ears or two eyes. Care for the leather, fondle it often; better for hides, a rubbing with oil, than neglect, desiccation.

Cousin for cousin, as once lay their *fathers*, brother for brother who knew the same woman, a woman who lay with two brothers, the fathers of these the two cousins. She lay with them both and found them the same, loins of like measure. How could she be blamed? No stranger had worn her, altered the garment, ruined the shape. She was true to the body, brother and brother, the two are the same, only the rank is at odds. I emulate her, her deed I have done: Atreus Thyestes, brother by brother; Agamemnon Egisthus, cousin by cousin, the same generation, branches alike in their firmness and bent, alike in their thickness and length. Agamemnon the son of that Atreus, Egisthus the son of Thyestes. Brothers and cousins, they own things in common, use the same vessel. One wears the shoe or the glove of the other, wears the same robe, the same Clytemestra. The lioness mates with the lion near by.

The glory of woman, her morning complexion, takes it from men, their strength for our beauty. Corrupt them with pleasure, tarnish their mettle, deplete them of vigour. Who rules the household and governs the kingdom? Let the kingdom be queendom, the mistress the master.

[A chariot from a byway enters the orchestra, Agamemnon and Cassandra, borne by armed men (there may be other armed men alongside); Clytemestra speaks now to Agamemnon:] Hail, human inhuman, mortal immortal; hail,

manly of men, godly of gods. Sovereign of air and of fire, despot of water and earth. Suzerain of above and below, for ever your glory and power. To you are these burnings, accept our oblation, we adore you and beg for your blessing.

Agamemnon, muscle and bone, strength in will and desire; hail, sword for my scabbard, dagger for sheathing, fill me with strength, with your love and your fibre.

Here is the hue to my cheeks, the lustre my tresses, here is the warmth to my breast. Waiting for twilight by day, wakeful by night for the dawn, nakedness wanting and wanting. Emptiness, fullness: emptiness, loins with desire; fullness, the heart with affection — full with a love for my god, Agamemnon.

The final assault on the city, the slave you have brought me, to pain at my pleasure, to scar for my healing, I straightway will teach her the custom: the higher the lower, the gentler the rougher. How grateful I am for this trophy, for havoc of woman on woman, my part in the spoils and the mayhem. Come, monarch of monarchs, dismount from the carriage, unbind the sandals that fit you as I do.

[Clytemestra, still at the middle door, to her women:] Impotent slattern, lay out the weaving, his emblem before him, a thoroughfare fine for a god. Let him ruin the scarlet and crimson. A path for a god, or a shroud for a prince on his bier. *[The women lay cloth (a grandiose white lion on a crimson background) to the door; Clytemestra stands just to the side, as if compelling Agamemnon to do her will.]*

[Clytemestra again to Agamemnon:] Comptroller of gods and of men, creator despoiler, tread it in triumph, rape

the rich threading, deflower its worth, ravish and ravage.
Then bathe away care, I will robe you in honour, and share
in the bloodshed. Brutal my love for the lion.

[Agamemnon:] Wife of my bosom, whom all things were
done for, all that is done, I am humble to fates that were
kind, in grief for my comrades, many by land or by sea.
Such grandeur I would not, a path to destruction.

[Clytemestra:] The work I did aching and numb, knowing
that men give their life. In your absence my mirth was to
plan for this moment. Boast for me, swagger, be hostile,
defiant, be bloody.

[Agamemnon:] I fear the resentment of hell and of heaven,
the grudge of the furies. If evil befall me, I spatter your
ledger, my life your account. *[With a characteristic
gesture, Agamemnon walks upon the cloth into the middle
door; his men, with the chariot, leave along a byway, as
the guard of Egisthus (the same men) will do later in the 1st
play and then again in the 2nd.]*

*[Clytemestra to Cassandra, moving towards her and also
towards the women's door:]* Gem for abrasion, the door
you must enter, the portal of captives, awaits you impatient.
Look again at without, then forever within. *[Clytemestra
steps back into the house by the women's door, followed by
her women; Cassandra and the old men remain.]*

*[Cassandra crying aloud, not noticing the old men, but
seeing the furies on the roof (the audience too sees them,*

for a moment, but the old men do not — as at the end of the
2nd play, when Orestes sees the furies, and the audience
does too): in delirium but not chanting:] The furies, the
horrors that shatter the ear with their screams and foul the
nose with miasma. Festering wounds on the eye, blasphemous shrieks become flesh, vampire fang at the veins.
[Now the furies are out of sight; Cassandra continues:]
What realm of the damned am I at, what household of
torture? A haggis of parts, touching and throbbing, abattoir
of the child, blood on the earth, the wall suppurates with its
filth. Mark them carousing, the furies, with goblets of
lymph and of bile, laughter for tears, gargoyles that drink
on the roof.

   [The furies appear again; Cassandra continues:] Have
you hearts made of clay, that you see and not flinch?
Lampreys that bore on the bowel, maggots that feed on the
brain. Nettle that crowds out the rose with fragrance of
corpses decayed. *[The furies are now gone from the sight*
of the audience, until Orestes sees them (as the audience
does) much later; but Cassandra as if she were still seeing
them continues:] Toad cabbage leaves that blacken by day
and whiten like graves in the dark, sins breeding like
fungus on logs, pods that swell in the marrow and burst.
Spider-bud roots infecting the bricks with contagion, doors
of corruption, courtyard of plague, fountain that plays with
despair.

   [Cassandra now sees through the wall of the house and
looks within (an effect in symbol, repeated through Pylades
in the 2th play); chants:] The bull is loose in the labyrinth,
heavy the stones, hammer upon them, torment lading his
death, the double-axe falls. In the labyrinth loose is the

bull, broken the stones, hammer upon them, his death fraught with torment, the double-axe fell.

Male wisdom of strength, female yielding in pain; female his yielding in pain, male her wisdom of strength: the bull has been gored by the cow. So tells you the Sun through his priestess, the Sun that sees all in his eye.

[The old men, severally:] Delirium, madness unfair to the truth. Dry is the palace, no blood on its dust. Incense and unguent, vigil and vow, rite read forward and backward, all has been cleansed, the crimes were atoned for, the ancient forgotten. What of the labyrinth bull, crushed in the stones, the stones in their sac like twins in the womb, heavy and crushed by the hammer upon them? Are you a gypsy, who knows the unknown?

[Cassandra, speaking:] What was I saying? the speaker who spoke was not I.

[Old men:] It was you to the sight and the hearing.

[Cassandra:] Not myself but the god that was in me.

[Old men:] Why should he talk of such things through your mouth?

[Cassandra:] The Sun who sees all has made love to my body.

[Old men:] The Sun is your incubus lover? and you are a witch?

[Cassandra:]   Cassandra his priestess, a virgin to men.

[Old men:]   What you tell, it is lies; I cannot believe it.

[Cassandra:]   No-one believes me: his will, that they cannot.

[Old men:]   If the god is your lover, why would he harm you?

[Cassandra:]   I take him within me but do not respond.

[Old men:]   What response does he want, the god in his glory?

[Cassandra:]   Trembling and shudders, of woman to man.

[Old men:]   Blasphemous talk of the Sun our pure light.

[Cassandra:]   His desire is for living: all that answer him flourish.   But mine is for death: a priestess of ice, the god's by betrothal, yet not fully his.   I am shy to love in the flesh and would not be immortal.   *Let* him protect me no more: I divorce him forever.   My robe that was his, I take from my bosom.   Ripp'd be the veil, broken the wand; the garland of flowers, sign of the flower I brought him, *they* shall be shattered instead, scattered and strewn.
    I enter the palace and shambles a priestess no longer, no longer a princess, nor have I tomorrows.   But the crimes that shall be, they know their own likeness, and the likeness

shall bring them to mind. Time rides a wheel and returns where it was. *[Cassandra goes into the women's door.]*

[The old men, on stones, debate what to do:] Demons enter our thoughts, make themselves one with us, but who has the Sun for her lover? A damnable word, that Apollo would break through her loins, would enter her womb with his radiant presence; the lie will be punished. And grim will her days be on earth, as a thrall to a crippler, the fell Clytemestra. I pity the plight of Cassandra, no longer betroth'd and protected, aloof from the god, a leaf to the gale.

Our queen lies abed with kingdoms and empires, but lain with a god has she not. A vixen made jealous, clawing her rival and prey. She will labour the girl to the bone, prod her from rest, starve her from bread, give her water polluted that gripes in the gut. Nor ever permit her the sunshine, her god.

[A groan from within the house, and then another; the old men speak by turns:] Was it the king Agamemnon? Was it the king or another? Was it from pain or exhaustion? What harm could ever befall him? Old wounds open up in the bath. Old scars cry out in the heat. Surely the queen Clytemestra? *Would* she be minded to harm him? Has a woman the strength of a man? The gods will protect their anointed. He might have been proud in his heart. Or said it was he and not they. The gods are resenting that pride. Is there a way we can break in and help him? The walls resist an assault. Our bones would break with our hearts. *[These 16 lines are to be distributed any way, or reduced, among the speakers (who number 12 or 8 or 6 or 4).]*

[The two-leaved gate is opened wide, upon Clytemestra and the bodies of Agamemnon and Cassandra, both covered in cloth uniformly crimson; the cloth that had been strewn is where it was; Clytemestra speaks:] I smote him three times for the powers that be, to thank them by book and by number; you twice heard him groan, for thrice did I wound him, the third left him silent. Three bites with the tooth I had whetted, for him and that slut of a trophy, behold them together, a blood-bond between them. Shorn of the stuffing to fill it, what use will he find for her vessel? What good is a wrapping with nothing to wrap? Mangled and ugly and lame, they limp through the regions below. Let his eyes remain open. And open his mouth for a cistern. All who bear grudges against him, who hold him to blame for our dead, come pour filth on his tongue *[she puts her hand to her rump and then on his lips]*. And that bitch without nipples, have the courage to handle her crotch *[Clytemestra puts her hand between Cassandra's legs]*, see whether the Sun left his ardour inside.

[The women, from the women's door, take the same abject position about the cloth as they had taken in laying it: this completes the death tableau.]

[The old men rising from the stones speak by turns to Clytemestra:] *[a]* If in your great double bed there was room for yourself and one other, why *he*, why *Egisthus*? *[b]* Why Egisthus who lingered at home, a woman whom you, as a man, work at will? *[c]* What is your love-making like, what perversion of parts? *[d]* Adultery, murder, one follows the other, I see it was needed: you *would* have been

punished, had truth come to light. *[e]* But the wrong man is dead, Agamemnon; the worse one, Egisthus, alive. *[f]* And why too the princess the priestess Cassandra, who saw her calamity written before? *[These six lines to be distributed with balance. The old men speak one by one; after each does so, he again sits on his stone.]*

[Clytemestra:] It is true that a woman, whose womb has been entered, bares hate towards a virgin, whom men would prefer. But that was no motive of mine, for a girl I could *be* if I wished, a maidenhead closing me off, the pulp of persimmon astringent constricting my loins. An innocence knowing no man and untaught. For so have I been before now, to nameless and numberless legions of lovers. Implanted small bladders of pig's blood within me, enclosing them deep in the scabbard, to bloody their sword. Do you say that I hated Cassandra? Not female as I am in body and mettle, not one to quicken desire or to *be* so belovèd in bed. I despised and contemned her, with pity not hatred. I killed her in kindness, her life had been ended. Some queens have levied their taxes in loving, fealty shown with the strength of the loins, or else amputation. I might have done such; but instead I was faithful, for I took to myself but the likeness, the very same kind as the other. Regent vicegerent Egisthus, for king Agamemnon, and who could distinguish between them, in stature or voice or in tissue and members? Cousin for cousin, alike as two peas of a pod. But the one burnt my daughter. Drag off the dead, sundered and severed, putrid remains, to the chamber of bones, where the hawks with clipped wings will clean the corruption. But damn'd be the soul, and

charms I will work for damnation.   *[She goes through the
wide gate, which closes, and her women take the cloth that
had been strewn, into the women's quarters, as the old men
in the 2nd will take it into the men's.]*

*[Egisthus (wearing the same robe as Agamemnon had
worn, but with a different disguising, the same actor with
the same armed men) comes upon the stage from a byway
(the men remain at the entry; the old men are still in the
orchestra), speaks:]* Now may the curse lie at rest that my
father, Thyestes, pronounced.   A regent as I am, he
honoured the sovereign as I do, at table and bed.   Then
Atreus his brother, the beast who begot Agamemnon,
pretended forgiveness, prepared him a banquet, gave him to
eat of his children.   As goblins they lurk in the palace,
fragments and remnants, howling and snapping, moan in
the night-time.   I, born the thirteenth *[or last, or whatever
ordinal is one more than the number of those in a group]*,
only I am alive, and the duty upon me, the deed I was
sworn to, is fair as can be.   I shared in the vengeance,
unwilling or willing, and now it is done.

Seed of my own I will plant in the warm moist earth
Clytemestra.   Make sterile the fruit of the seed she was
sown with before.   The lion majestic in mane and in might,
he ruins the cubs of the lion preceding.   *[Egisthus enters
by the men's door; his actor returns presently as Orestes
from a byway; the guard leave as the men of Agamemnon
had done and as they will leave when Egisthus enters the
house in the 2nd play; these armed men will enter presently
from a byway as the followers of Orestes.]*

[The old men, in the orchestra:] Is there justice on earth? Clytemestra, Egisthus, burn them in Tartarus, justice condign and ex*qui*site. The rule of the kingdom, the empire, is theirs, is theirs for the time, may it not be for ever; and we who are brittle in bone, brittle and aching, obey them unwilling. May Electra be blest, wipe the tears from her eyes and the grime from her skin. May Orestes an exile return. Dead is our lord Agamemnon, avenge him Orestes, come prince to our hearth. Wherever your dwelling, Orestes come home. *[The old men, huddled, leave along the same byway as the guard of Egisthus had left by, humming some of these final words, though not in unison.]*

[This is the end of the 1st play, continuous with the beginning of the 2nd:]

[As the last of the old men leaves, Orestes enters the orchestra from the other byway, accompanied by Pylades, and by followers (the group of armed men, somewhat differently dressed or disguised); with Pylades, who stays a few steps behind him, Orestes goes to the altar (which is now the tomb of Agamemnon), and leaves a token of his hair; speaks:]

[Orestes:] I lay this hank of my hair on the earth of your tomb, king of kings Agamemnon my father, the son of Atreus ruthless king of kings, and Pleisthenes and Pelops kings of kings, and Tantalus who ruled when time was new. My father Agamemnon, king in the war over Helen, the bride of the king Menelaus your brother, and sister to

bitter-as-gall Clytemestra my mother. You see that the hair
was your own at my age, so you know that Orestes, his
hair and his hands and his heart, is coming with vengeance.
I swear by Apollo, our lord god the Sun. *[He steps back;
speaks now to Pylades:]* It must be Electra *[he leads
Pylades to partial concealment, around the corner of the
wing or onto the byway].*

*[Electra comes with women who bear pitchers of different
sizes and shapes, all from the women's door, slowly
towards the tomb; the women sing, not in unison but one by
one:]* Drugs from root and from pith, drugs that soften and
soothe, drugs forgiving the past.   Pods of sarcophagus
blooms, transmuting the carrion calyx.   Honey from
meadows of witchwood and webworm, Lethe-bank wort
soporific to grudges.   Tuft of new fleeces to soak up the
bitters, petals like seashells that hear and forget.

[Electra:]   No, darlings, do *not* pour the gruel, the
libations, the drugs that you bear in the pitchers.   Do *not*
keep the mission to quiet the shade of my father — to sleep
him with wine and sweet unguents.   For here is a hank of
raw hair like to mine, and if mine it is not, from the head
it must *be* of the one whom I love as no other, Orestes.   An
anthem of joy.   I taught him to weave this braid of the
kingdom, and tie the knot of our clan.   Oh my brother
Orestes, the underworld aid him, his heart and his hands.
Oh ghost of our father belovèd, of king Agamemnon, smart
with your pain, that your malice may double our strength;
oh bleed below ground, oh do not be soothed with libations.
[To the women again:]   No, by the wall of the palace go

empty your pitcher. And those that Egisthus would claim as
his cause, the furies, the terrors, lull *them* to sleep, to *them*
sing your song, make somnolent *them*, but our father keep
wakeful. The masonry parched will drink up the brews and
at once become drier than dust.

*[The women leave the grave and move to the house and
pour their libations on its walls, chanting as before:]*
Drugs from root and from pith, drugs that soften and
soothe, drugs forgiving the past.   Pods of sarcophagus
blooms, transmuting the carrion calyx.   Honey from
meadows of witchwood and webworm, Lethe-bank wort
soporific to grudges.   Tuft of new fleeces to soak up the
bitters, petals like seashells that hear and forget.

[Orestes comes forward:]   Electra, my sister.

[Electra answers:]   Orestes?   The body I knew every inch
was a boy, the body I knew with my touch and bathed with
my kisses, it seems a moment ago, but you are a man.   Let
me look at your eyelids and earlobes, and handle your scar.
You whom I love.   Our mother and that which she takes to
her bed, they put you in exile, they meant in safekeeping.
I feared it was so; I thought you were gone from my life,
the life of a woman in bondage, but now you are here.

[Orestes:]   A man in all of my parts but most in the
strength of my will.   With Pylades speaking for god as the
Sun.   I laid on the grave the pledge of my hair.   Tell me,
why have you come, and the women as well?

[Electra:] *They* know better than I, for they sleep by the vixen our mother, but I in a dungeon of chambers below.

[Women, severally:] Yes, truly your sister is more of a slavegirl than we are, as threadbare her clothing as ours, and as meagre her meat, by rule of the harsh Clytemestra. Who awoke from a dream with a gasp. Some demon or fancy had torn the soft veil, she thought Agamemnon, unquiet below. With pitchers of drugs have we come, as she bade us, embalming the shade. But Electra, afraid until now, found courage in you; she *told* us, do *not* soothe his wounds, but comfort the furies instead, the furies, the children who drink on the roof, carousing all night and all day in their parties of blood, and moan as they trade with each other their organs and tissue. Your father is wakeful and aches with dishonour. Avenge him, Orestes *[the women enter the palace by the women's door]*.

[Orestes to Electra:] Will our mother not know me? She thinks me a boy of no beard and no fibre, a boy with the voice of a girl; but *still* she may make out the signs, though she never has looked at me closely, as you my sister have done, my Electra, who know all my mind and my body. I will speak with the speech of a stranger from far-away mountains, the lilt and the click of a man from the heath *[Electra enters the women's door]*.

[Orestes calling out at the men's door:] A stranger and friend, let me make myself known, I was given to visit the house, told by the prince of a welcome.

[Watchman comes through the men's door, speaks:] Your name? and where from? and what is your want? The house bars its doors to the world. We live to ourselves and *if* we have secrets we keep them.

[Clytemestra at the middle door:] This is no inn to the needy, no comfort to homeless and hungry. Alms to the destitute, beg for them elsewhere. The dogs at our doorstep, they earn all their keep or they starve.

[Orestes:] We are three in the peaks and the valleys. I Rhada*man*thus the hunter, with Pylades priest of the Sun, but the third is not with us, Orestes, our friend whose delight is the harp, and his paints, and the incense more fragrant than heaven. He offered us lodging and gave me the robe as a sign you could trust us: ought we to tell him your welcome was cold?

[Clytemestra:] If Orestes would have you, this house is your home. A bath for your bones, a feast in your honour. Enter in safety, your tendons relax, now slumber your eyes, all fears lay aside, all cares and all weapons. If you leave with regret I shall rue my lost chances. *[To the watchman:]* Give them soft bedding and open the hearth for a burning *[Clytemestra enters the middle door]*.

[Orestes to the watchman, as Pylades and the followers enter the men's quarters:] Is my father awake? are the furies benign or malignant? Will Apollo as lord god the Sun bathe my hands with pure light? *[Orestes enters after the others.]*

*[As he does so, out come the women, by the women's door,
and speak one after another:]* I dread to say, our mistress
wants Egisthus.   With his men or without?   To what
*in*human end?   To un*do* the defenceless, mayhem of host
against guest, or for pleasure in pain?   Do they hunger,
the furies? Our lord must be brought, or again she will whip
us, with pulling of nails and of teeth.

    *[Electra comes out from the women's door; the women
say to her:]* Our lord must be brought.   Where *shall* he be
found, by the swamp or the pits?   Is the guard a-march on
the road, or stripped and wrestling with blades?   I fear as
a woman to see them, or let them see *me*.   They are
stallions and bulls, though more brutal.   They think I am
made for their use — not pleasure but wrenching of muscle,
competing to ruin and rip.

[Electra:] This is the hour when they scrape off the scurf
and anoint themselves for the War god. *I* will go *with* you;
the rapist would not ravish *me:* though a drudge I am half
Clytemestra.   I will say, Come alone, prince Egisthus, the
guard is not needed.   *[Electra goes by herself to find
Egisthus; the women flutter about, sing their song Drugs,
and then enter the house by the women's door.   At the
same time, Egisthus comes from a byway, with his guard,
but then he enters alone by the middle door, with the
gesture, at the last moment, that Agamemnon had made
upon entering; his guard at once leave as in the 1st play.
And soon: a groan or cry from within, the voice of
Egisthus or of the servant.]*

[A servant comes out by the men's door, and speaks:]
Murder! Break down the door, smash with a ram, get her
out. Murder! I could do nothing *[he enters by the men's
door, just as Clytemestra comes out by the women's].*

[Clytemestra:] Why the shout through the ear of the house,
what cause is there now?

*[Orestes comes out a few steps at the middle door, Pylades
behind him; Orestes speaks:]* Egisthus would have you
come join him, great queen. *[Clytemestra goes towards
Orestes; he continues, to her:]* Yes, I am Orestes.

*[Clytemestra sees what he intends; she strokes or fondles
her breast (the erotic gesture, here shocking, is repeated in
the 4th play, but is appropriate there); speaks:]* Before
you would hurt me, remember my breast. You were a
newborn, afraid and unhappy; I gave you my milk.

[Orestes:] Pylades, priest of Apollo, look for the Sun, and
say can I harm her, avenge Agamemnon?

*[Pylades, seeing the murder of Agamemnon (in symbol), as
Cassandra had done, and repeating her words in the same
voice, chanting:]* In the labyrinth loose is the bull, broken
the stones, hammer upon them, his death fraught with
torment; the bull has been gored by the cow. *[No longer
chanting, but in the speaking voice of Cassandra:]* I see on
her breast the touch of Egisthus. Her nipple is hard as they
geld Agamemnon. *[Pylades to the side prays to Apollo and
enters by the men's door, as:]*

[Orestes to Clytemestra:] God has told me my duty *[his arm about her, they enter by the middle door (the same gesture, same actors, as in the 4th play, but there, with Menelaus and Helen, it is a gesture of love)].*

[Women come out by the women's door, into the orchestra, where they remain, perhaps kneeling between the stones; they speak:] Why the shout through the ear of the house? Do they hunger, the furies? The curse, will she surfeit the curse? Are the furies benign or malignant? Ugly as hate, do they hunger?

[The wide gate opens upon a death tableau as in the 1st play except that Orestes holds a solid-colour crimson robe on his left arm as well as a sword in his right hand; he speaks:] Together on earth, together in hell. Rhadamanthus has brought them to justice; now, underworld torment, the tongs and the pulley, the blade and the screws, Clytemestra, Egisthus, accurst, unforgiven, the dungeon of pain, and forever. Agamemnon, the soul of my father and wraith, you should know that Orestes has wrought the revenge. Your bones will be honoured, the shades will respect you.

    [Orestes calls out to old men (the same group as in the 1st play) from round about; continues:] You who dwell round about, who knew Agamemnon, my father, now look at the robe he was killed with, she kept it a trophy of games, the robe he had worn to our glory; stretch it out, see the lion, where *is* it?

    [As he speaks, the old men he has summoned enter from a byway, onto the stage, stretch out the robe, and take

an abject position beside it, as the women at the close of
the 1st play had done. This completes the second death
tableau. The déjà vu effect ought to be stunning.]

   [Orestes continues:]   His blood has covered the
emblem, the blood of the lion, the sign of the lion, the cloth
is my witness, the force of his body is here, the proof of
the crime.

[The women, still kneeling in the orchestra, speak:]   It is
like as it was, the curse on the house; and what pair will be
next — Orestes, Electra? — to lie as these lie, as the others
once lay, Agamemnon, Cassandra.   Menelaus and Helen,
the same true for them? does the past breed its image? will
today be tomorrow?   The tracks of the doom, I follow them
hardly, the lair of the beast, it is hidden *[the old men take*
the robe through the men's door — as in the 1st play women
had taken it through the women's].

[Orestes:] I kept my oath to Apollo, our lord god the Sun.
What his *will* was, I asked of his priest, of his Pylades,
friend and most holy.   Was the woman who bore me and
nursed me the one who would kill Agamemnon? was *she*
the hyena whose nipple was hard as they gelded his body?
The agent of health, who has told me my duty, was priest
to the light of the day.   *[Orestes sees the furies, and so*
does the audience, but not the women in the orchestra (as
in the 1st play). The furies are now in the courtyard, as if
from the corpse of Clytemestra (but they are the same, to
the eye, as the children on the rooftop in the 1st play;
Orestes continues:] What horrors come *at* me, the shades
of my mother. Apollo, protect me. *[The furies chase*

*Orestes along a byway; as soon as they have left the
courtyard, the wide gate closes behind them.]*

*[The women, in the orchestra, rise and sing or hum their
song, though as if distraught:]* Drugs from root and from
pith, drugs that soften and soothe, drugs forgiving the past.
Pods of sarcophagus blooms, transmuting the carrion calyx.
Honey from meadows of witchwood and webworm, Lethe-
bank wort soporific to grudges. Tuft of new fleeces to soak
up the bitters, petals like seashells that hear and forget.
*[The women enter by the women's door — so ends the 2nd
play — while:]*

*[Orestes — here the beginning of the 3rd play — pursued by
the furies, along the other byway than the one he had fled
by, comes into the orchestra; believing he is within a
temple or shrine of Athene, and grasping at something (or
nothing) that he thinks to be her emblem, he prays to her:]*
Athene, daughter of God, I implore at your image. The
furies, the horrors, the wraith of my mother made many,
would have me for mayhem. But truly I killed her by word
of Apollo.

[Furies dancing around Orestes, hand in hand:]
A circle without an escape,
     from claws woven inward or out.
Transfixt with a spike through his butterfly heart,
He sees what is *not* but is blind at what *is*.
A circle without an escape,
     from claws woven inward or out.

[Furies change direction, now counterclockwise:]
Wheel backward, reverse and revert;
   undo, twist off, pull apart.
Turn blood into urine, and urine to dung,
Turn dung into worms with a plug at the arse.
Wheel backward, reverse and revert;
   undo, twist off, pull apart.

[Furies menace Orestes, dancing in- and outward:]
Too late to regret or repair;
   too late for bad into good.
Now travel the meaningless journey of torment,
Now scream through your hide from the breakage within.
Too late to regret or repair;
   too late for bad into good.

[Athene, entering the orchestra from a byway:] I felt his
hug at my emblem; I come in response to his groan. From
this bondage of mayhem release him; I give him the
freedom to cling to my likeness. No-one shall harm him
unless he is guilty. I ask for the judgement of judges, a
jury of elders; and then we shall see. *[To persons
thereabout, who are summoned as in the 2nd play — but
now into the orchestra, not onto the stage, and who sit on
stones as in the 1st:]* You there, I would like you to help
me, *what* you think best in this cause. Did he do what he
should not have done? did he act with clear conscience?
Or neither or both or some other? The case will be argued
and then you will vote. The decision is yours if you reach
one; if not it is mine.

[Athene acknowledges Apollo, who has just come from a byway:] Lord Apollo, my lord god the Sun, have you come to Orestes? Reply to the furies who want him, to mar and dismember. They speak for a moment; you answer as briefly.

[Athene continues, with a recital of history:] When Helen was taken, unwilling or willing, an army made war, Menelaus her husband by law and a king, Agamemnon his brother the king and commander. And him, Agamemnon the king, Clytemestra the sister to Helen, she killed him homecoming. Orestes their son then avenged him, acting with cause as you said to . He acted with cause but perhaps not enough. That is the case to be pleaded and heard. And these judges, not I, will give judgement. *[Adjust the following, for 12 or 8 or 6 or 4.]*

[Furies, one after another:] Accurst, for a crime that dishonoured his mother. *[1st juror raises his head in the gesture meaning no, frowns, and shows a closed fist as a sign of hostility.]*

[Apollo:] Absolved, for he honoured the name of his father. *[2nd juror bows his head in the gesture meaning yes, smiles, and makes an upward movement of the hand, palm open.]*

[Another of the furies:] Accurst; he was curdled and formed in the churn of his mother. *[3rd juror like the 1st.]*

[Apollo:] Absolved; as infused by the vigour and vim of his father. *[4th juror like the 2nd.]*

[Another fury:] Accurst for shedding the blood of a kinsman. *[5th like the 1st.]*

[Apollo:] Absolved, for the blood of a kinsman impelled him. *[6th like the 2nd.]*

[A fury:] The blood of his mother cries vengeance for justice. *[7th like 1st.]*

[Apollo:] The blood of his father cried blood in requital. *[8th like 2nd.]*

[A fury:] Should one who commits such an act go unpunished? *[9th like 1st.]*

[Apollo:] Should one not perform what one sees as one's duty? *[10th like 2nd.]*

[A fury:] The deed is so awful we heed not the motive. *[11th like 1st.]*

[Apollo:] Whatever the deed, he should have a clear conscience. *[12th like 2nd].*

[Athene:] The ballots are equal; so here is my judgement. When votes are a tie, to condemn or release, you acquit. You may call it the vote of Athene. Orestes goes free, your goddess has willed it. The session is closed.

[Furies:] Shame on the earth and its gods. You trample the law into mire. Specious and counterfeit coin. Where

is decency now, where the straight look in the eye, where the firm grip in the hand, where is the faith of the lover, where is the trust of a friend? Why should we value the truth?

Release the vials of plague, may weeds crowd out the grain. Dry and cold the winds that blow, nor olive thrive nor the grape, nor ewe bear forth her lamb. Moaning and groaning and howling and tears: these are the songs you will sing. Happy the dying to die, sorry the living to live.

[Athene:] No, you are guards of the good, and all who are speaking of strength, of character, fibre and pluck, shall think upon you and your sign. At the sacrosanct heart of our land will your grotto be honoured, and those of high office will swear on your name. Beholden to you shall we be, and you will be gracious to us.

[The furies, not having listened, say again:] Release the vials of plague, may weeds crowd out the grain. Dry and cold the winds that blow, nor olive thrive nor the grape, nor ewe bear forth her lamb. Moaning and groaning and howling and tears: these are the songs you will sing. Happy the dying to die, sorry the living to live.

[Athene, repeating herself:] No, you are guards of the good, and all who are speaking of strength, of character, fibre and pluck, shall think upon you and your sign. At the sacrosanct heart of our land will your grotto be honoured, and those of high office will swear on your name. Beholden to you shall we be, and you will be gracious to us.

[Furies:] Lady Athene, tell me again. What honour and rites would you give us?

[Athene:] Those who bear witness, or plead in a cause, will invoke you to hear them, and *if* they are false it will be at their peril. And when we pour out the wine of libation, or burn the lamb of a feasting, a portion is yours before ours, a drop and a morsel. Pledging ourselves at a wedding, to one and no other, all *that* will be done on your name, the well meaning Eu*men*ides.

[Athene claps silently, her attendants appear; she speaks:] Women, my darlings, belovèd, who care for my temple and altar, come clothe our fair sisters, *put* on their shoulders a raiment of crimson and scarlet, the hue of the blood that the clan spilled aforetime, but the hue and the cry of high honour besides.

[Athene claps silently again, armed men appear; she continues:] And men in armour with torches, guide the procession below to the shrine of the tombs, the home of our sisters and friends, the well meaning Eumenides, kindly disposed towards the city and country, benign and benevolent.

[Athene addresses the group of jurors:] And you who gave judgement, who saw the two sides of the drachma, *you* lead the way. I am *with* you, Athene your goddess. Apollo the sunshine is with you as well. And Orestes the prince now the king. Sing a hymn for today and forever, a hymn to the blessèd well meaning Eumenides. *[Procession leaves gravely, along a byway, with humming, but promptly: so ends the 3rd play].*

*[Proteus, from the other byway than the procession of the
3rd play had left along, with sacks over his shoulder, lugs
a vat to the altar in the orchestra, stirs the vat (which emits
smoke or mist, not much), and speaks with mime and
dance:]*   A broth that turns men of due parts into
greybeards, and greybeards to satyrs who dance the
sikinnis, and satyrs to men of due parts; chrism and
smearing and slime; now wicked now sacred, now horrid
now jolly; congealing to scabs, dissolving to spittle; three
slimes and three smears and three chrisms; the balm a slug
exudes to smooth his plodding, the mucus lodged in
vesicles of mallows, the lava throbbing from erotic dreams;
chrism and smearing and slime; this lore I tell as a wizard
and faun, where fauna deflower the flora; you know me as
Proteus the blue man with dolphins, or Bacchus the green
man with grapes.

*[Armed men, from the byway the procession had used, come
into the orchestra; speak one by one:]*   The delicious
aroma blisters our tongue. We come here bedraggled. The
southwest wind and the south wind wrestled like giants; the
waves were a juggler with ships. Menelaus our lord at the
tiller, and Helen our lady below, the woman the cause of
the war, whose rape he avenged when they burnt down the
city, or was it a willing abduction? We fear they are lost
in the storm. Agamemnon his brother, Clytemestra her sister: the nobles of earth, and their households, in glory and
power, dishonour and mayhem, how close the resemblance,
their houses, without and within, same post and same lintel,
for brother and sister. Have we come to our home? The
landmarks are strange though familiar. The pathway is

gone, the field overgrown, but the cut of the rock, the edge
of the shoreline, are all as they were.   The cobbles feel
right to the foot.   *Red* stones and yellow, procession of
lions inlaid, a procession to palace and temple, one upon
one upon one in a march through the city, their features
alike and their style, couchant and rampant and regnant the
lions, and brutal from father to son, brutal the lion, the
lioness brutal and cunning.   Would you nourish our heart
with your broth?

*[Proteus, with mime in the theatre, or in shots if on film, as
he speaks of his shapes — a dragon (not a bull, since that
is on his costume), a whirlpool of sulphur, a blanket of
flame, a barleyfield ripe:]* Chrism and smearing and slime;
it makes me a bull or a dragon, a whirlpool of sulphur, a
blanket of flame, a barleyfield ripe for the locust: those are
my shapes.   A broth that turns men of due parts into
greybeards, men into greybeards, men . . . into . . .
greybeards.   *[He offers the ladle to the armed men, who
drink, then twitch or huddle and enter the house by the
men's.   At once, by the middle door, old men — seemingly
the armed men transformed — come out, dance with
tottering step (as in the 1st play), and sit on stones (as in
the 1st and 3rd).]*
     *[As they come out, Proteus continues (before his
rigmarole becomes tiresome, its method of utterance should
be changed, from speech to chanting or humming, or the
tempo should be changed, as Beethoven syncopates the Ode
to Joy); by the time he is half through, or two-thirds, the
old men are sitting on the stones:]* Three slimes and three
smears and three chrisms; the balm a slug exudes to smooth

his plodding, the mucus lodged in vesicles of mallows, the
lava throbbing from erotic dreams; three spokes to the
wheel, from alpha to beta, to gamma to alpha revolving;
threefold the charm from the county of morphs, as weapons
are numbed but again are made fearful, as loins become
limp but again stiff and stark, as days amble slowly while
lives run a-gallop; three slimes and three smears and three
chrisms; a broth that turns men of due parts into greybeards, and greybeards to satyrs who dance the sikinnis,
and satyrs to men of due parts; from alpha to beta where
loins become limp, where days amble slowly while lives
run a-gallop; a broth that turns men of due parts into
greybeards, and greybeards to satyrs, greybeards to satyrs,
greybeards . . . to . . . satyrs. *[Proteus gives the ladle now
to the old men on stones, who enter the house by the men's
door. At once, by the middle door, satyrs — seemingly the
old men transformed — come out, and dance rather as the
furies in the 3rd play had done.]*

*[While the satyrs dance — at some length, for this is a
satyr play — Proteus continues, singing and humming:]*
Three slimes and three smears and three chrisms; the balm
a slug exudes to smooth his plodding, the mucus lodged in
vesicles of mallows, the lava throbbing from erotic dreams;
a broth that turns men of due parts into greybeards, and
greybeards to satyrs who dance the sikinnis, and satyrs to
men of due parts; from beta to gamma, the weapons made
fearful, the loins that were limp made again stiff and stark,
the conscience in thrall to the rule of arousal, display of the
force of his forebears, or thrust of his issue; the greybeards
to satyrs who dance the sikinnis, and satyrs to men of due
parts. *[The satyrs drink from the ladle, and then go in by
the men's door.]*

[Proteus continues:] Chrism and smearing and slime; from alpha to beta, to gamma to alpha revolving; satyrs to men of due parts, to . . . men . . . of . . . due . . . parts; the brew is exhausted, the kettle is dry; the satyr exhausted is man in return to himself. *[He leans with both arms against the vat, and will not now be seen at once.]*

[Helen and women with pitchers enter from a byway into the orchestra, as in the 2nd:] I have found the right path, my right home, thanks to heaven. The petals I nurtured, the grasses I tended, not just as they were, but almost: generation begetting its image: the bottle-bouquet and the windstar, the bell-of-the-moth and the cottonwood fluff, all bloom on their grandparents' grave. *[She sees him; continues:]* And here is the green man, the blue man, the wizard I sang for, singing my song at his grotto *[Helen begins to touch his robe, his hand, his cheek]*, beseeching him forth, to teach me the art of mixing his drugs with my beauty, what balm for the eyelid and earlobe, for fragrance of whisper and lustre of lip, and how I should comfort the torment of men in their pain of desire.

It was here that I came for you, came with my women at solstice for Bacchus or Proteus, the changer who changes his name and his colour, the green man or blue man, who changes for better the women who kneel at the loins of his emblem, and take him within them. *You* are the goblin, the warlock, the friend to the witch. Is there *one* of you only or many? They say you are legion. I know of your spells, conjurations, taboos, of your sorcery, miracles, magic.

Today is the solstice, and now as aforetime, the women have come to adore you. I embrace them with aching of pleasure, awake from an *un*happy dream, let it fade with the night in the day. But my lord Menelaus, who kept me below, he is mindful to shame me by custom. My tresses, like poppies for red in the starlight though blueblack as night in the sun, he will shear to the bone, and the yoke for the pair of us, emblem of marriage, of trudging together, he means to asunder.

Come, Bacchus and Proteus, come lord of the hues that are soothing and kind, enchanter alive in the woods or the seas — whose forested grotto is green with the emerald, whose cave in the blue of the ocean is wondrous for sapphire, secluded from *those* blind with doubt, but discovered by faith, with drugs for needs and desires — with your favour now bless me. Affection is yours for a kindness. All manner of plant owes its pollen to you, all species of brutes owe their jism. Be good to me, green man or blue man, and brew me a potion, brew a love potion, we gathered the makings, this bark synergetic with blossoms: though mild one by one, they have power together, a catalyst each to another; they multiply strength, and do *not* merely add. Help me in kindness and give him to drink, a recipe mother to daughter, she told me its potency lasted a lifetime and longer — told me the man that I want would be potent as well, potent through *his* life and mine and beyond, as after our living on earth he would lie with me always, his body in mine. The broth you were seething, the broth that bewilders the air hereabouts, put it by and concoct my elixir, and give him to drink. Not a metamor*phos*ing from greybeard to satyr, but a rousing of love with desire.

[The women (not Helen) pour from the pitchers into the vat, and speak as in the 2nd play:] Drugs from root and from pith, drugs that soften and soothe, drugs forgiving the past. Pods of sarcophagus blooms, transmuting the carrion calyx. Honey from meadows of witchwood and webworm, Lethe-bank wort soporific to grudges. Tuft of new fleeces to soak up the bitters, petals like seashells that hear and forget.

[Helen enters the house by the women's door, as Proteus stirs; the women fill the pitchers and enter the house by the women's; Proteus speaks or hums at least part of their song, and then adds a phrase of his own:] Drugs that soften and soothe, drugs forgiving the past. Pods of sarcophagus blooms, transmuting the carrion calyx. Honey from meadows of witchwood and webworm, Lethe-bank wort soporific to grudges. Tuft of new fleeces to soak up the bitters, petals like seashells that hear and forget. Let it *be* a love potion, let the man love the woman, let the man love the woman, not harm her.

[Menelaus comes into the orchestra from a byway:] These dunes and these rocks, the seaside and meadows, they must *be* my fair hearth, the earth I would kiss in my gladness. The gables and roof, they are surely my house: home is the worn Menelaus. Tempered my courage and sinews; *now* may I rest from the wars. A leader in arms, but the plaintiff, a man in disgrace. And the heavenly Helen, the hell in my life, I would shame her by custom, by right and by duty. For *if* there are gods, they rebuke me. If destiny cast

me an eon ago, the mould was ordained ruination. An itch in her flesh was the cause, a worm in her body.

[Proteus replies, with mime or film shots, as before:] This empire is Egypt, and Proteus the changer am I, a bull or a dragon, a whirlpool of sulphur, a blanket of flame, a barleyfield ripe for the locust. The trough in the sea must have turned you around, that in thinking you headed for home, from the sea in-between lands, you headed away. The sun has come up in the west, it shines in the north at the noonday. Your bearings are lost, you stumble, a stranger. Nor *are* you a gallows of justice, a sceptre of shaming by custom. Sojourners are welcome, but not their resentment. Refresh yourself with a sip of the broth, Lethe-bank wort soporific to grudges.

[Menelaus drinks from the ladle, and turns towards the middle door, where Helen appears and addresses him:] Menelaus, muscle and bone, strength in will and desire; hail, sword for my scabbard, dagger for sheathing, fill me with strength, with your love and your fibre.

[Women come from the women's door as in the 1st play, and Helen speaks to them:] My darlings, lay out the weaving, his emblem before him, a thoroughfare fine for a god. Let him ruin the scarlet and crimson. I would he might ruin my body as well.

[Helen again to Menelaus:] Brother to king Aga-memnon but greater, more potent, if what my fell sister, the harsh Clytemestra, once told me is true; for she warns all the world that will hear, as a man he is lacking endurance and moment; but you are a thirty-years oak in the girth of

your loins, the cone and the magma of mountainous
dormant volcanoes erupting, the blast and the suck of a
cyclone that burrows a deep in the earth.   More kingly
majestic by nature than he, Agamemnon, as I am less
haughty than she, Clytemestra: we match them without and
surpass them within.   Oh heart of my heart, bed-*fel*low I
long for, trample my love, the cloth that I made with my
hands when the hands could not *touch* you.

Comptroller of gods and of men, creator despoiler,
tread it in triumph, rape the rich threading, deflower its
worth, ravish and ravage.   Then bathe away care, I will
robe you in honour, and share in the bloodshed.   Brutal my
love for the lion.   Come *in*to our house, I will sponge away
anguish, and come into me, for the unguents of healing: the
cure for your aching and grief is held in the hold of my
body: come *where* you belong, the part I am lacking, make
haste and then linger.

[Menelaus before cloth:]   This purple you wove but to use
up the time, I walk on it not as a prince in a triumph, I
walk as a bridegroom defrauded, who finds that the bride
is a whore.

[Helen again to Menelaus:]   I resonate now with a thrill to
your voice even speaking reproof.   The song of my loins
takes its rhythm from yours, let us sing to each other as
man within woman, and shout a cascading of music that
deafens the ears and the eyes and the sense.   *[Now with the
same erotic gesture as Clytemestra to Orestes:]*   Before
you would hurt me, remember my breast. You were the first
one to gaze on me naked, to touch me without and

within. Whenever they took me by force, when they gave me a pleasure I hated, you were the body I felt, the god that came into my innermost being. My hazelnut eyes I shut tight in their shells, my legion of captors I shut in the dark: it was you that I saw in my mind and to you I responded. Others may say they have known me, have known my ripe bosom and belly; to me they were all Menelaus, to you were my tremors. Come darling and prince, reach my heart from my womb. The stain of my *un*willing whoredom, cleanse it away, to make me a virgin again. The purple I wear as a woman, the scarlet and crimson, strip it with love from my body and cast it aside, clothe me in white, to make me as clean as the snow, as clean as the cloth on our couch, cloth that has never been lain with. *[They enter together by the middle door, his arm about her as Orestes' was about Clytemestra (same gesture, same actors), but now with love not with force. The women (who, as the wives of the armed men, will presently appear in the courtyard, when the wide gate opens) take the cloth through the women's door.]*

[Proteus alone, stirring vat:] Drugs that soften and soothe, may the past be forgiven, tuft of new fleeces to soak up the bitters, petals like seashells that hear and forget, droplets of ardour, of strength and affection, call to your fellows, empower the blood and the brain, empower the lungs and the loins, all is forgiven forgotten like yesterday's dream; let it be a love potion, let the man love the woman, not harm her *[the vat foams violently]*.

[The gate opens wide (for only the 3rd time: the first two were the death tableaux); Menelaus is as before, but Helen wears a white tunic or frock showing her (beautiful) breasts, and a white chaplet; the actors smile for the first time in the four plays; the same for the armed men (their spears laid aside) and the women, now rewedded, who leave the courtyard and enter the orchestra, the wide gate closing behind them.   They dance around Proteus, chanting:]   Two halves are united, man and woman together, to Apollo and Bacchus the glory, and thanks for our love.

Apollo & Bacchus

Overview and Synopses, *Edipus*, *The Women of Bacchus*

Apollo is the god of harmony, of healing, and of prophecy. Bacchus (Dionysus) is the god of fertility; drama arose from the worship of Bacchus, and the plays are in his honour. *Edipus* has to do with Apollo; *The Women*, with Bacchus; but the power of both gods is in both plays, as in ourselves.

The two plays may be regarded as versions of extant masterpieces. They are also like papyrus finds of disputed authorship. Might not Thespis himself — who came from a locale devoted to Bacchus, but who dramatized other matter as well — have written them? Or Choerilus, who with a hundred sixty plays won thirteen victories? Or Pratinus? Or Phrynicus, who was by reputation, among those of his time, the greatest of all?

Aeschylus wrote an *Edipus* as well as a *Nurses of Dionysus*, a *Women of Bacchus*, and a *Pentheus*; Sophocles wrote not only two plays about Edipus but also a play about Dionysus; Euripides wrote not only *The Women of Bacchus* but also an *Edipus*. And besides the work of the three immortals there were plays in the fifth century about Edipus by Meletus, Achaeus, Nicomachus, Philocles, and

Xenocles, and plays about Bacchus and his women by Iophon, Xenocles, and Polyphradmon — and plays in the 4th century about Edipus by Carcinus, Diogenes, and Theodectes, and a play about Bacchus and his women by Cleophon, to say nothing of Chaeremon and Timocles. (See the second appendix in Haigh's *Tragic Drama of the Greeks.*)

So many plays about Edipus! so many about the women of Bacchus! No doubt some of them had much in common, but they must also have had elements of originality. Similarly, though between the drama surviving from antiquity and the plays printed here there is much in common, the two here also have something original, something unforeseen.

Faithful translations tend to become unfaithful. For if the Greek dramatists changed old stories to make them new, but if what then had been made new has become old again — if we have read a play or heard much about it — if what was to be unexpected is now expected — our experience in the theatre is utterly inauthentic. We honour Apollo and Bacchus more highly by restoring some of the surprise enjoyed when the enactment of myth was in its heyday.

Each of these two plays, *Edipus* and *The Women*, is an entity complete in itself, with its own urgent, continuous action and its own set of correspondences. But the two are meant to combine well, with each other and with the plays here following them, into one entertainment.

Edipus in the first play, the Prince in the second, will be acted by a man; the Prophet in the first, Bacchus in the second, by a man or by a woman in transsexual disguise.

Edipus and the Prince may even be, though of course they need not be, played by the same actor, and likewise for the Prophet and Bacchus. Between Edipus and the Prophet, as between the Prince and Bacchus, there is a stark physical contrast — say, thick and thin, white and black — to heighten the effect when the one takes the place of the other.

For the sake of the effemination scene in the second play, the Prince and the other men are bearded, though Bacchus not. The Prince and the other men have shaggy hair and may be of a craggy general appearance; their cloaks are homespun, nondescript, with a cord or belt at the waist; their shoes are rough, with leggings; the men, except for the Prince, also carry spears; he wears a gold dagger. Bacchus and the women wear dresses (his, yellow; theirs, white, transparent or opaque), with a cord below the bosom; their feet are bare. In addition, Bacchus wears a lynx hide and a pendant with a large letter B. He also carries (or wields, or brandishes) a large pinecone on a rod (described as a fennel stalk); so do the women, after the effemination of the Prince and before the cataclysm; and so does the Prince at the end, when he appears in the garb of Bacchus.

Because beards are a sign of maleness in the second play, Edipus and the other men in the first play, the Prophet among them, are bearded too. Edipus and the other men, though not the Prophet, might in fact have the same general appearance and clothing as the Prince and the other men in the second play. Edipus bears a sceptre as an emblem of rank. The cloak of the Prophet is threadbare and mouldy.

With his staff, he is a tripod, as Edipus is at the close. The Theban has some infirmity and his looks may be distinctive in some minor way besides: he could have an animal hide about his shoulders, though not one so gaudy as to make the lynx of Bacchus less striking. The Queen wears a yellow transparent dress, showing her beautiful breasts; her women wear white; and she alone wears flowers.

Each of the plays needs a group of twelve (or eight, or four) — six men and six women (or four and four, or two and two) — though for some of them transsexual disguise, again, would not be undesirable. The members of the group may vary in size, race, and age. Much of the group's movement is recurrent (as shown here in italics):

In the first play: 3 men and 3 women, or 2 and 2, or a man and a woman, *lament ritualistically*; an equal number join them; later, half of the (6 or 4 or 2) men in the larger group, and half of the (6 or 4 or 2) women, *leave with the Prophet*; the remaining half of the group then *speak in double time and move in a pattern*; much later, this remaining half, joined by the Theban, *lament ritualistically, speak in double time and move in a pattern*, and then *leave with Edipus (who now resembles the Prophet)*.

In the second play: 6 men and 6 women, or 4 and 4, or 2 and 2, are on stage; *Bacchus chants 'Women take Bacchus' and dances away, and the women dance after him*; later, a guardsman comes with Bacchus; the Prince dismisses the men and the guardsman; Bacchus *sings 'The lynx'*; the women return and *sing 'The lynx'*; half of the women follow Bacchus, the other half remain with the Prince; by and by, all the women gather together and *sing*

'The lynx' once again, while eating from their hands; *the Prince (now resembling Bacchus) chants 'Women take Bacchus' and dances away; the women dance after him.*

In the first play, half of the Group (6 or 4 or 2) leave with the Prophet, touching his garment, and half leave with Edipus at the close, similarly; in the second play, half of the women (3 or 2 or 1) leave with Bacchus, and all the women (6, 4, 2) leave with the Prince at the close. In this manner the movements may be (but need not be) stylized between the plays.

The palace, within the city walls of Thebes, is the background for both plays. The performing area may be either rectangular (proscenium) or round (arena). No more than one door is used and there is no glimpse into the interior of the palace. Nor is there any décor (except that on film there may be spectral shots: for *Edipus*, of a sphinx and a griffin; for *The Women*, of a bull and a python). The seven gates of the city, if shown, are open for *Edipus*, closed for *The Women*. Besides the door, there are entrances from (or exits along) byways to the left and the right: the exodus of the Prophet, and then of Edipus, is along one of them. The recessional of *The Women* may be similar, or may be through the nave, or central aisle, of the theatre.

Edipus and *The Women*, with *The Duel* and *Odu*, are parallel to the version of *The Oresteia* between these covers, and might be offered with it in a two-night festival. Essentially the same cast and costumes would be redeployed, the second night, though *Edipus* and *The Women* have a single group each (of twelve at the most), whereas *The Oresteia* needs no fewer than four groups (which might, in a grandiose production, likewise number as many as twelve each). The music would be the same, between *Edipus* and *The Women* on the one hand and *The Oresteia* on the other, and so would some of the choreography. The stage building, a palace, is the same as well, except that for *Edipus* and *The Women* only one door is used and the interior is not seen, whereas for *The Oresteia* three doors are used and the interior is twice revealed as the gates are opened from within. No properties are needed for *Edipus* and *The Women*; but a broad layout of gaudy cloth, and a circle of stones around a sunken altar, are needed for *The Oresteia*. All in all, the theatricality — of recurrence and metamorphosis — ought to be about the same.

The Sphinx

The Griffin

Synopsis of *Edipus*:   Men and women of Thebes lament to Apollo, because of the plague.   Edipus curses whatever polluter is to blame. As an adventurer some years ago he had come from Corinth against the sphinx and had solved her riddle — partly by thinking of his own infirmity (the reason why he was named the man of swollen feet), and partly from seeing the Prophet go about on three legs, as he continues to do: there he is now. Edipus tells of the present miasma — the griffin — and of its gasp 'Not strike where you were struck, nor enter in the door you came from'. The Prophet speaks of training in anguish, directs Edipus to look within for the meaning of 'not strike nor enter', and warns him against bestial violence, bestial lust.

As the Prophet leaves, some of the Thebans follow him. The others say he was of no avail against the sphinx and is of none now against the griffin. It is Edipus whom they admire, and the Queen as well, who has just come nigh. Edipus recounts to her that he had been told by the Prophet that he would bring death to his father and lie with his mother. She explains the threat away, and Edipus agrees that he cannot be at fault, either for bestial violence, since he had bettered the sphinx without mayhem, or for bestial lust, except that hardly a word passes between the Queen and himself. She replies that her silence is from old grief for her firstborn, who had been taken as an offering. She adds that her former lord was killed on a highway; for the thought has come to her, that the body might have been left unburied, which might be the offence to Apollo and the cause of the plague; to probe that fear she has sent for the servant who was driving the carriage. Edipus tells that he killed a man on a highway himself, though the body of *that* man cannot be the unclean thing, for vultures consumed it at once. The servant comes, remarking upon the name, the man with swollen feet, which reminds him that he took the Queen's firstborn as an offering and pierced the ankle bones, though he then spared the child and gave him as a foundling; the Queen enters the palace. The servant continues, it was to a great house in Corinth that he gave the child; Edipus enters the palace. The servant, wondering whether the Queen needs him further, enters the palace. Presently, he returns and tells of the tragedy. The men and women lament. And now Edipus appears, a tripod like the Prophet and seemingly his replacement in wisdom and suffering.

Bacchus
from a Vessel in the
British Museum

Synopsis of *The Women*: Bacchus — in a yellow dress,
wearing a great letter B, barefoot, and with a pinecone rod
— comes singing and dancing among the people. The
women follow him, the men remain. The Prince, coming
among the men, tells of disgust at the beguiler, and wants
him taken captive. A guardsman comes with Bacchus, who
is hardly a captive, though, for no bonds can hold him. To
keep the men from being corrupted, the Prince dismisses
them. He then questions Bacchus about his power over the
women, and asks what the women do in their orgies.
Bacchus says, with song and dance, that the Prince, if
effeminized of his beard and in attire, could see for himself.
The women, now with the pinecone rod, return, singing a

A Woman of Bacchus
from a Vessel in the
Fogg Art Museum
at Harvard

song of Bacchus and glad to have found him again —
doubly glad because (with the effeminized Prince) he is
double. As they sing his song, they caress each other (and
perhaps fondle animals besides). Bacchus dances away,
and some of the women follow him; the others caress and
fondle the Prince: if they find he is still a man, what will
they do to him? After signs of a cataclysm, all the women,
now without the pinecone rod, singing of Bacchus and with
morsels of prey in their hands, gorge themselves senseless.
Almost at once they awake, remorseful that they may have
killed and eaten not a beast, but a man. By and by, though,
the Prince appears, in the yellow dress and with the letter
B, singing the song of Bacchus, and the women follow him.

Edipus

*[In the background, fires burning, sounds of sorrow. Three
men and three women, or 2 and 2, or 1 man and 1 woman,
on stage, lament in a round:]* Apollo, your beauty the
sunshine, my heart in the dust.

*[Three other men and three other women, or 2 and 2, or 1
and 1, arriving one after another, say by turns:]* My
mother is dead, my father, my sister, my brother, my
daughter, my son, and the joy of my life and my reason for
living. The *first* day, the body is blue as the lilac; the
second, as green as the clover; the third day, the body is
ulcers. Physicians who balm with an ointment are faint
from the stench of their patient. The boils pullulate on a
network of fissures, the innards peep through them, a hag
from a curtain. The soul is a-flown like a bird when its
cage is left open; the body she loved is as hateful as vermin
that twitch. When the dead are repugnant, you burn them
at once, and lament them tomorrow; the dying you hurry
along to the hospice and read them the book of the doom.

[Those who were first on stage continue lamenting:]
Apollo, your beauty the sunshine, my heart in the dust.

*[Edipus comes out from the palace, says amidst the whole
of the group:]* I curse the polluter of Thebes, that man or
that woman to blame, whosoever pollution incurring his
wrath turned Apollo against us. I curse the polluter, the
tree and the seed: may his daughters not marry but age at
the loom, may his sons make war on each other.

[The whole of the group say after him, in a round:] May his daughters not marry but age at the loom, may his sons make war on each other.

[Edipus:] I saved you before, I will save you again. *[With eyes to the sun:]* Lord Apollo, you gave me the answer before, now give it again. I am Edipus king of the Thebans, my heart in the dust. *[To the group, though hardly aware of them:]* The sphinx, the lion marauder, the face of the priestess who speaks for Apollo, the lion marauder besieging the city, besieging the Thebans and Thebes, allowing no travel or commerce, an island in seas without ships, the face-of-the-priestess marauder that muttered a riddle and crippled the failure to answer. I heard of the sphinx, the felon marauder, the ogre, her fame had reached Corinth, my homeland and princedom. I came as a man among men, with bravado to try her. I answered the riddle *Who walks on four legs in the morning, on two at the midday, on three in the evening?* She melted like butter, the sphinx in vexation and shame. I had answered her riddle by making a good of my bad, with the help of a man in the distance.

[Someone from the group:] A man in the distance?

[Edipus:] I thought of my name as I do every day, of my name and the bones of my feet, I was wondering *why* I was such as I am, with a body that differs from others, a matter I think of in silence, a matter I thought of each day of my childhood, not asking the parents I loved, from the fear it would hurt them to tell me, but asking myself. Had a harm befallen my body before I could walk?

*[The whole of the group, first one speaking, then another,
staying respectfully distant from Edipus, not touching him,
nor kneeling to him:]* We could see that the name was
a true one, and yet we were slow to address you as
such. That is *why* you have found us aloof; but in truth we
adore you, who did for us more than another. Your
commons, till now, has kept to its place in the market; we
know that the commons and king are not peas of a pod; but
now facing *death* we have come to your steps. Our sister
and brother are dying, our mother and father are dead;
intercede for our daughter and son.

[Edipus, unaware of the group:] I thought of myself, by
the word I am called from the knobs at the joint of my
ankles, the knobs I am known by and named for, the
socketed balls of my shanks, in the clasp of the hinge at the
heel, the *ed* of edema, the swelling of dropsy inherent
unchanging, the *ed* of a lifelong edema, edema the swelling
you see in your Edipus, ankles a-swollen, edema. The puss
of the platypus, octopus, foot. A name for a man who has
feet that are swollen, your Edipus. Better than no name at
all, *swol*len *feet*, but not what a man would have chosen.
*Finger*claws or *hairy mole* or *warty nose* or *run*ning *sore*
or *swol*len *feet*. Are they names to be called by? The *ed*
of edema.

[Someone from the group:] We would give you the name
of all that is best under sight of Apollo. *[Another from the
group:]* Our word as your name is *triumphant, immortal*.

[Edipus, still unaware of the group:] The *arth*ra, the
socketed balls of my shanks, as *if* they were big against

nature. The socketed balls for my coupling, the arthra of
chronic arthritis, perpetual pain in these arthra, a pain but
one *not* of the body. In truth they are healthy, my ankles,
as firm as a mountainous oak. Were they growth of the
bone from a harm? the profusion of strength from an
injury? Arthra that tell of my lot, of a hardship before I
had come to awareness? But firm and my pride, though
inhuman in size and my shame, the mark of a beast on the
prowl from the tundra, these arthra, the mark of a beast or
a giant or god, the sign of the strength of my thews, and an
envy to men in their hearts, and to women a cause of
desire. Call me Edipus, *swol*len feet, *call* me by name, and
remember the arthra, the socketed balls of my shanks, of
my ankles, the arthra that give me command of the earth.

[One or more from the group, singly:] You have reason
for pride; we were shy to say aught of the matter. Aloof
you will find us no longer: our life in your keep.

[Edipus:] I saw myself crawling, and saw myself standing
as well. *Who walks on four legs in the morning of life, but
on two at the midday?* Myself as I *had* been and was,
though the rest of the riddle was baffling.

[One or more from the group, singly as before:] Our
Thebes is your homeland adoptive. You came as the
riddler who bettered the sphinx, and we made you our king,
we would *have* you as *god*. For you rescued the city,
though many were gone. And those that were left are now
dying by will of Apollo. Would *you*, as our *god*, intercede
with the sunshine?

[Edipus, still unaware:] Every day, every hour of the day, by obsession I thought and I think of myself, I reflect on myself, as crawling and standing, on *four* legs or *two*. But *that* was not all, would have *not* been enough, but as *if* by an omen from heaven a man with a staff had appeared in the distance, a man whom I often have seen even now, while trudging his way with a staff, through the market and ramparts, as *if* that support were a part of himself. Now the answer was whole, the ages of man in the riddle *Who walks on four legs in the morning, on two at the midday, on three in the evening?* I answered the sphinx and her riddle; she melted like butter. The answer was *I* as I *had* been and *was* and would *be*. He was I, that man with the staff, a-trudging his way, a-trudging his way on three legs in the evening of life.

[The whole of the group:] The prophet is wandering still, outside of the walls and within them, the mendicant seer, going daily about for his alms, giving warnings, the prophet, the mendicant seer whom the sphinx was afraid of, aware of his knowing. They *say* that he bartered his manhood, the stones of his loins, for the arts of Apollo. And *if* you would *speak* to him, *there* he is now.

[The Prophet, seemingly blind, a tripod with his staff, with disgust at a stench:] Faugh!

[Edipus and the Prophet behave like mutually repelling particles that stay a measured distance from each other; the group remain, unmoving and still; Edipus:] The city is

open, the seven gates wide, for clean blowing air to disperse the miasma, the gasp of the griffin, the griffin that glows like the will-o'-the-wisp, the meadowfire floating, the gasp from the lungs of the lioness hawk, the beak of the hawk that belongs to Apollo, the gasp of the griffin *[the gasp may be heard now and afterwards from time to time].* The plague that we die from, by will of Apollo, malefic the griffin with hideous gasp.   Not stalking, besieging, no danger out*side* of the walls, like the sphinx, for the griffin leaps *on*to the walls, and then she leaps down and within, and the gasp is her message, the griffin that mutters in sounds having meaning though hardly.   I *just* make them out to be saying: *Not strike where you were struck, nor enter in the door you came from.*

[The Prophet:]   As the sphinx, so the griffin.   Lioness body, the sphinx and the griffin, the face of the one like the face of a woman, the face of the other a hawk.   As with *one*, with the other.   Corruption offending Apollo, pollution uncovered, some body unburied, some filth or some tumour, or *cov*ered pollution, a secrecy vile but unpunished; take heed of Apollo.

[Edipus:]   The sun and the moon — as a prince and a *prin*cess, as brother and sister, by day and by night — ferry death with their bows and their quivers of arrows; their name is destruction to men and to women.   Or strumming their bow like a harp they make music; the world is a garden of goodness and mirth; for the god is a healing physician; the law is a kingdom he governs, and time he brings round as he will; the art of the sculptor is his, and

the art of geometry; problem and paradox, riddle and answer, Apollo our lord god the Sun, his servant is Edipus.

[The Prophet:]   *Know yourself*, that is the first of the mottoes, the rule of Apollo.

[Edipus:]   I study my body to learn why I am as I am.

[The Prophet:]   The second is *Naught in excess*. You have come to be king; beware of the height.

[Edipus:]   The third and the last of the words of Apollo, incised on the wall of his temple, the plain letter *R*.   The ascent of his mountain is painful, but *then* the pure air is a tonic that freshens the body, the temple is wine to the soul. But the plain letter *R*?   Is the meaning *You are*?   Is the sense that you *are* but a man, not a god, but a man, nothing more?   I have thought that the *R* might mean *arthra* for me, or the socketed balls of my ankles, affliction and strength.

[The Prophet:]   The words of Apollo, incised on the wall of his temple, *Know yourself*, and *Naught in excess*, and the plain letter *R*.

[Edipus:]   The arthra, the socked balls of my ankles.

[The Prophet:]   In the *R* is the answer why Thebes is a hospice for sick and a house of the dead.

[Edipus:]   I will search out the cause of the plague; I unravelled the deadly conundrum before, of the sphinx, and

she melted like butter; so now will I answer the griffin.
Are you feeling the shape of the entrails — the liver and
kidneys, the heart and the spleen and the filth?

[The Prophet:]   They tell me the shape of the future.

[Edipus:] Did they tell you the lore of the sphinx? Were
you *ab*le to salvage the city and *would* not?

[The Prophet:]   The riddle of four legs, of two, and of
three, in the morning, at noon, in the evening. The end is
in *me* as I *am*, as in *you* by and by, of no *worth* to yourself,
nor of worth to a man in your limbs, nor of use in your
stones to a woman, but crippled and ruined and broken in
arthra, undone; for the riddle was wrought from your life as
the heavens foresaw it. The sphinx was the first of the
troubles to make you a prophet, the one to replace me, a
seer who can *look* through the dark at the core in its
glowing, when all are benighted a seer who can witness the
sunshine; the sphinx was the former, the griffin the latter:
the riddle imposed by the sphinx, enigmatic the gasp of the
griffin. The training in anguish continues, the training in
anguish.

[Edipus:] If the sphinx was my training, I welcome the
griffin, miasma, the gasping, the withering gasping, a death
to the plants and the flocks and the people, breathing her
breath with a whine, and as *if* with the words *Not strike
where you were struck, nor enter in the door you came
from.*

[The Prophet:] Inquire in yourself of this plague, of the groan, of the howl, of the gasp.

[Edipus:] Rigmarole words in the gasp, not strike where I was struck, nor enter in the door I came from. What use is your counsel? I thought you might see as a blind man the things unseen to our sight. But instead you have told us my training in anguish continues.

[The Prophet:] *Pollution of bestial mayhem, pollution of bestial lust.* The seer to replace me should look to his hands and his loins. As before you could see what was meant by the sphinx, so again you should see what is meant by the griffin. The gasp would have meaning for *you*, for yourself if not for another.

[Edipus:] Bestial *mayhem*? You say that I slaughtered the beast? She *lay* down in homage, though once she had torn half the city. She melted like butter, in homage to *me*; and as lord of the sphinx, as the saviour of Thebes, I ate of that butter, I tasted her mana, I supped on her power, the sphinx is with*in* me. I Edipus king of the Thebans subsuming ingesting the sphinx in my body; what *she* was I *am*.

 Bestial *lust*? Do you say I make love like a beast, that I lust without thought of the vessel? They *say* of your*self*, that your manhood is broken. I challenge Apollo to show my perversion. *Not* as a beast do I lust but as heaven intended. I have lain as a god with a goddess desiring. The god of the Sun is my witness.

[The Prophet:] In your arthra discover both power and fault.

[Edipus:]　The socketed balls of my shanks with edema, inhuman in size and my shame, like the arthra, those others that turn at a swivel, a pivot, in *me* though in *you* not again, the socketed balls of my loins, the arthra implaced in a pouch at my fulcrum, the arthra I hold in my scrotum, now hidden but told of and famous, my manhood more precious than pearls of great size, and a legend they were in my boyhood, my shame but my glory, the weight of my power, a ram or a stallion, like stones from the ice age, these arthra, begrudged me by men but the joy of the woman who knows me. *Is* there a channel between them, from ankle to gonad, from *this* pair to that pair, from arthra to arthra, the socketed balls of my body?

[The Prophet:]　Not strike where you were struck, not enter in the door you came from.　Look to the blood on your hands and say *who succeeds while undoing success*, succeeds to the throne while undoing success in succession; look to the seed you have sown and then answer me: *when* is a daughter three quarters her mother, and when is the half of a brother the son?

[Edipus:]　Are they riddles from nature? Some bee or some ant that does *not* make a couple as we do?

[The Prophet:]　Was the sphinx not a dream?　Who else of the living has seen her?　And who through the day or the dark has laid eyes on the griffin?　Who *else* could be sure they were beasts of Apollo?　Do you know in your heart they exist?　By and *by* all will *come* to you; *then* will the griffin be gone like the sphinx, the gasp evanesce, and *I* will return to my grotto for ever.

[Edipus:] Are you death after life or the life after death? *[Edipus and the Prophet have moved so that Edipus is now in the background, the Prophet is close.]*

[The Prophet:] I foreshadow yourself; this day is my last, I am then with Apollo, and you will be me. *[The leaving of the Prophet along a byway, with half of the group, who touch his garment, is highlighted, for it will be repeated.]*

[The remaining half of the group, in double-time overlapping speech, with movement, as at the close:] The prophet and mystic and seer, he can *tell* from the entrails the shape of tomorrow, but offers no help for the present, no more than he did in the past. He might as a wizard have saved us, the sphinx went a*bout* and besieged with her jest and devoured us. And today he might save us, the griffin who warns with a gasp, *not strike, nor enter. If* he can *tell* from the entrails, why *could* he not tell from the sphinx, why *can* he not tell from the griffin, and *if* he is *ab*le to tell, why *does* he not help us? *He* is a beast of Apollo, a sphinx or a griffin, himself, and a riddler. We sense there is sanctity *on* him, we touch at his holiness, *thread*bare and mouldy with stench from the entrails; but Edipus *you* are resplendent, for *you* meet Apollo as equal, and *you* we regard as a god. *[The Queen enters from the palace, the group continues:]* And the lady our sovereign, your woman unhappy, unspeaking, adorable, she whom we love and would bring to a smile if we could, is resplendent as well, with a beauty unaging from heaven *[the group remains but now is silent as before]*.

[Edipus to the Queen:] He told me the sense was, *not* to
bring death to my father, nor lie with my mother. Bring
death to my father and lie with my mother. I would in a
dream, where the laws of our waking are loosened and all
may be done. If the sphinx was a dream, if the griffin
today is a dream, then I am a nightmare, a horror that men
would forget if they could. In a dream as a boy I brought
death to my father, a combat of man against man, unaware
it was he whom I struck with my cudgel; remorseless, for
dreams are a realm without conscience; on waking I looked
at my hands with a terror of dread.

   In a dream as a boy I have lain with my mother, for
dreams are a realm of voluptuous carnage; I knew in my
heart it was she though the face was not hers nor the
breasts; they were *yours* in their beauty, the beautiful
breasts of my kisses; I entered the womb I had come from,
knowing and wilful and thick with desire; but on waking I
asked if I would, and my answer was never. The parents
who reared me in Corinth, my father and mother, the king
and the queen of that land in the south and the sun of
Apollo, are safe from my bestial mayhem, my bestial lust.
The danger is merely a dream or a myth.

[The Queen:] The mendicant seer is a hoax and a humbug.
He *meant* father*land*, mother *tongue*. You *have brought
death* to your father *land* adoptive, death for the buttery
sphinx; you did *lie with* your mother *tongue*, when you said
that you *were* but a man among men, merely one like
another, for that was a lie. Oh how vague and surreal, the
words of the prophets! You *are* not a man among men,

merely one like another, the first among equals. But gold against earth, you are gold thrice refined in a furnace with bellows, or gold that was struck by a coiner of shekels, and struck in a mint nothing *like* any other.

[Edipus:] Not strike where I was struck, nor enter in the door I came from. Not strike where I was struck; you say I was struck in a mint. The Prophet has told me, but told me untruly, of bestial lust and of mayhem. My bestial mayhem — I conquered the beast without bloodshed or bruising, the sphinx merely melted, a pool of raw yellow. My bestial lust — my love for your beauty is not like the lust of a beast; it is worship, though worship in silence; no word ever passes between us.

[The Queen:] No word is between us. My life is a thing that I *would* not remember. I married as soon as the form of a woman was *on* me, my lord had just grown to a man; and I *see* him in *you.* Our wedding was happy, to each was the other's desire. But the law of the land for its queen, that what opens the door of her womb, as the firstborn, is given to heaven, a gift to the gods for the sins of the kingdom — that law for the queen but no other — was sorrow not *just* for a time, as they said it would be; that grief was a sorrow for ever. My firstborn was taken, the joy of my life. Then the love that I owed to my lord, the desire for his body, to make him a child as replacement, was gone. I would eat in despair, nor sleep without weeping, nor speak in a voice that was steady. And *if* I am taciturn still, without words as we love, that has *come* from my pain.

[Edipus:] I would suffer as you do. The custom, the queen should surrender her firstborn, and give him to heaven, that law is a crime and the throne is not worth the commission.

[The Queen:] My lord came to death on the roadside, from cutthroats and robbers, with only one witness, the faithful chief servant, — that servant had taken my firstborn and afterwards tended my forest of sorrows, the grove where I wander at morning and evening, — he crushed for my lord the raw vintage that furthers forgetting, and thickened the wine adding mushroom hal*lucinatory* with spice from the lands of the *day*break, and unguents that balm away grief for a solace in lieu of a marriage, the winepress of drunken escape for my lord from a woman in tears, — that servant had harnessed the horse for the carriage and driven my lord to his death, he was injured himself but then afterwards healed in a house below earth a long summer, and *when* he saw *you* on the throne and all well, he retired to the uttermost end of the kingdom, now living a hermit and meagre. That servant I sent for; I thought that the corpse of the king might have long been unburied, a cause of offence to Apollo or such. No doubt my good servant will banish those worries away.

[Edipus:] I my*self* killed a lord on the road, and with right, when his horse and his driver would run me to earth, or tumble me over the cliff, on a pass where the footing was narrow. That lord on the roadway cannot have been *he*, not *your lord* left unburied; the sky had been dark with ashen grey vultures in wait for a boar or a goat that was stumbling, ashen grey vultures in famine, and *now* when

the lord and the horse were both breathing their last, the birds fell at once upon *them* instead of the boar that was living though hardly; they fell on the lord and the horse, for the flesh, bones, and all. The poisons within them, the poisons and malice and pain, of the lord and the horse, were digested and ground to a powder. The driver was gone still alive. And no-one remains to the winds from that mayhem unburied offending Apollo.

[*The Queen:*] When you came to the kingdom and throne, for slaying the sphinx, and looking like him whom I loved to begin with, it seemed a return to the time when my firstborn yet lived; I was loving again as before, I was loving my lord but in you as his likeness, and almost as *if* you were part of myself. Only *you* take my thought from my firstborn. And *that* is the reason I *want* you within me so often so much [*she puts his hand to her breast*]. I am lonely this moment, our flesh is not one, return to my womb with your body. For *now*, like a queen among bees, with sons and with daughters from you, I would *bear* more and more, to comfort the ache for my firstborn. Oh fill up the emptiness now, I want you within me, the place of my firstborn. The thought of the child makes my temper too heavy for talking. Return to my womb.

[*Edipus:*] The prophet has told me besides that the sphinx was a dream, or a myth, and the griffin the same.

[*The Queen:*] A meaningless riddle, the ages of man; for what is the meaning of life? Was the sphinx, is the griffin, a dream? the sphinx, the griffin, a myth? Is not life but a dream we are glad to awake from? fulfilment of things we

desire, fulfilment of all that we dread? I have lain with my
firstborn — my son grown to manhood — in dreams, as my
longing for him took the form of desire in my womb, a
desire he would *come* back with*in* me and give me his love.
Was that dreaming my life in a myth? Is it true that a
wrong is requited in dreams, that a debt is repaid beyond
measure? Come, be one with me now, in a bed strewn for
love and for dreams.

*[The Theban servant arrives, and addresses the Queen, in
the presence of Edipus and the remaining half of the
group:]* My lady, they tell of your *un*changing beauty,
forgotten by me like a spectre or wraith; I should *nev*er
have known you, nor anyone else; my senses are numb
from a blow to the head by a felon I met on the road, time
ago. Your messenger gave me a summons, the palace of
Edipus, name of a man who has feet that are swollen. A
wheel comes around like an ox at a grindstone. That day,
when your firstborn was taken by custom, the duty was
mine of enchaining the socketed balls of his shanks with a
spike, at the joint where the long bone is hinged with the
heel, and I injured the beautiful boy as you bade me,
though wishing instead I had cut off my hand. It is strange
how the matter returned. Let me say as a salve to your
grief that my own was too great. I went back to the bluff
where the boy had been left to hyenas, and took him away
to the southland. *[The Queen plunges into the palace; the
Theban continues, to Edipus and the group:]* A man and
a woman were wanting a child they might rear as their
own. In compassion, defying my orders, I gave him to
them as a foundling. Their home was in Corinth, a house
of great wealth. *[Edipus plunges into the palace; the*

Theban continues, to the group:] It is riddling and strange that your king is named Edipus. Woe to my head; I can*not* work things out; for the harm that was done to my skull by the goad, when the highwayman *struck* down your king of aforetime, and struck on the bone of my mind with his cudgel, that headache has clouded my brain. Let me ask of the household attending her whether my lady has learned what she wanted *[the Theban enters the palace]*.

[The remaining half of the group, singly:] What *was* the connection, the fetters, the foundling, the riddle, the king on the highway, the throne to our Edipus? What of the gasp of the griffin, the plague of miasma, the warning *Strike not where you were struck, nor enter in the door you came from*? The word of the prophet, what *was* it? The wish and the will of Apollo, what *are* they? Is life but a dream and a myth? *[The house lights go out briefly; a man's yell is heard; the lights come on, but dimmer.]*

[The Theban enters from the palace:] My lady is dead, her own *hand*. And when Edipus *saw* her he knew her as wife and as mother. He knew she was mother and wife in one person. And as son and as husband embraced her as both, in remorse and in love, and kissed her and fondled her body as mother and wife. Then he took from her bosom the daggers my lady was wearing, his hands at the amethyst handles, the daggers my lady would wear on her breast. With his hands on the handles he thought of his name, and the arthra, the socketed balls of his shanks, where the pin was that wounded the baby, the fetters that hindered his ankles, as *if* he were travelling backwards in time, a wheel

in reverse, and would chain them once more, with the
trouble he bore in his name, and would offer himself to the
gods, to hyenas and vultures, for training in anguish, a child
on the mountains; — but then changed the arc of his stance
and his purpose, to injure the arthra he held in his fulcrum,
the arthra impouched in the sac at his fulcrum, impaling
himself in the scrotum, to ruin the arthra, those others that
turn at a swivel, the arthra more precious than pearls of
great size and great splendour, the socketed balls of his
loins, where his strength was and dreadful begetting, the
testes, the testicles witnessing all he was fated for, socketed
arthra of past present future, to work a purgation of filth
from the city, to stab with the daggers the stones of his
manhood, to ruin himself for Apollo; — but then changed
the arc once again and *struck* on the third pair of arthra, the
*lus*trous *large black soc*keted *balls* of his *eyes.*

*[The remaining half of the group collapse at the news, and
lament as at the beginning, by turns, in a round:]* Apollo,
your beauty the sunshine, my heart in the dust *[and (with
the Theban) again heap dirt on their head; and say in
double-time overlapping speech, with movement, as at the
Prophet's exit:]* Our king and the prophet, our Edipus,
riddles of sphinx and of griffin, conundrums of four legs
and two and of three, and of striking where struck and of
entering *in* where he came from, of striking his father and
entering *in*to his mother, the riddles of sphinx and of
griffin, the jest of the one and the gasp of the other, a lion
with face of a priestess, a lion with face of a hawk, the
beasts of Apollo to try him or warn him, or make his life
all of a piece, like a dream or a myth, and ironic, with

training in anguish to fashion a wizard, a seer who can see-
without-seeing the will of Apollo, a dream or a myth of the
things we desire and the things we most dread to our father,
the things we desire and the things we most dread with our
mother, channels connecting the days of before and of after,
channels connecting the arthra, the arthra below, in the
midst, and above, ruination and healing and ruin again, and
the channels connecting the pairs of his arthra, all large
against nature, those channelways working to cripple his
feet and his loins and his eyes.

[More slowly:]   The plague evanesces, pollution,
corruption, the griffin has melted, her feathers dissolving to
dew, the city is clean of miasma, and bright as the heavens.
Our saviour has saved us again, our saviour named Edipus.
Dipping his hands in the melt, he made it a balm for his
body, he made of the griffin a part of himself, the griffin
and sphinx are with*in* him.   Our Edipus, swollen afoot as
he was for the glory of god — he is ruined for *us*, in his
arthra, the socketed balls of his feet and his loins and his
eyes.   As he looks on the face of Apollo, he sees through
the sun to the core of existence.

*[Edipus enters from the palace, blind, in the threadbare
mouldy cloak, a tripod like the Prophet, and leaves as the
Prophet had done, along a byway; the remaining half of the
group, with the Theban, follow him, touching his garment,
as the other half had done when the Prophet left; as these
leave now they say in cadence:]*   He is ruined for *us*, in his
arthra, the socketed balls of his feet and his loins and his
eyes.   As he looks on the face of Apollo *[music]*.

The Women of Bacchus

[Six men and six women, or 4 and 4, or 2 and 2, are in the orchestra or on stage, before a large house; his music preceding him, Bacchus from a byway chants, with dancing:] Women, take Bacchus with*in* you; women, take *god* to your body; women, old women, young women, half women — women, take *god* to your body, and give of your body to *god*. Women with milk, leave your sucklings at home, you may suckle the *god*, give your milk to the *god*, your breast in the mouth of his kindred, your nipple to fawn or to serpent.

The stalk of the fennel, the cone of the pine, the emblem of Bacchus, of man in his manhood, of man and of bull and of stallion and ram, of a man in the strength of the girth of his loins, when his energy flows from his mind and his heart to his loins, like a torrent in springtime, when conscience is vassal, desire suzer*ain*; I will teach you to brandish the stalk of the fennel, the cone of the pine.

Blessèd is time in destruction, blessèd is time when renewed, as the *year* comes around in a wheel, nor is time like an arrow, not forward nor backward but round and around, for destruction renewal destruction; the wild is a claw and a fang to the tame, you are leaving your houses and temples, your homes are the mountain, your altars the forest, your *con*jury north of the north wind.

Women take god in your innards, take god with devotion, pay homage, dismember the god and devour him, the god whom you suckled, your nipple to serpent or fawn; now devour him, his flesh and his heart and his loins, you are *one* with the god, he with *you*; come, be *mine*, come, be *one* with your Bacchus, devour him, be *one* with your god, come to suckle, dismember, devour. *[The song and dance will be repeated at the end; the women, touching themselves and each other, follow Bacchus (as if enchanted by him) along the other byway, and this too will be repeated at the end; the men remain, murmuring, their words indistinct.]*

[The Prince, from the house, comes before the men:] Has he escaped me? Your prince will defend both the state and its honour. That creature, with love in his lashes, enticing the women, telling them *do and be done to*, corrupter of chastity, blasphemous creature obscene and lubricious half woman himself, who would loosen our morals, I *want* him in bonds. If a woman is ever infected with pleasure, her duties at home are forgotten, she pauses in daydreams and never is pure in her body or mind as before. There is nothing she cares for but pleasure again and again and a pleasure again. All the orderly moderate calm of her life is diseased with the itch of desire. Let a woman know nothing of pleasure. That creature, corrupter who loosens our morals, I *want* him in bondage and put to the pain, that his sorcery charming the women, the art of his dance and his frolic, his music of timbrel and flute, may be *known* to us, known and undone. My guardsmen are seeking him out; they have *found* him!

[A single guardsman comes with Bacchus:] We captured the strange and half womanish creature and bound him in withes of the hemp as a prison, a beast that a captor was keeping on leash, but a shrug of his delicate shoulders has

rent them, a shrug of the green of his pinecone, the touch of his rod, and *here* he is free as the weather and hard to foretell.

[The Prince:] I was minded to hurt him with torture; it seems that he *can*not be hurt. He is panting but not with exhaustion. Away from this demon unholy unwholesome, for fear of the plague! He is frail but his manic and magical spell is a torrent of rain or a fire in a grassfield, and *you* who are strong as an ox would be weak as a prey. The blasphemous creature lubricious infects us, corrupts us, deflowers, dismembers, unsexes, unwomans, unmans. Alone he and I will take aim at each other and I will prevail with my armour and weapons of virtue. *[The guardsman & the men leave.]*

[The Prince:] What *are* you, dear fellow?

[Bacchus, dancing:] I am life incarnate — and death — and life reincarnate, god or year-spirit or Bacchus; my staff is a stalk with a *pine*cone, a fennel-and-pine ithyphallus with ivy, an emblem of life after death after life; I am teaching the women to flourish that stalk with its *cone* to bring *joy* to the loins of creation; my dance of the feet and the hands and the head, down the arch of the back through the innards, my dance is the spasm, the tremor of death or the shudder of life, the twitch of the heart as it stops or the pulse of the male and the female begetting.

[The Prince:] Year-spirit, is *be*ing your art, or be*com*ing, today or tomorrow?

[Bacchus:] All *things* change about and regain their old likeness, the flesh is interred for the worms, but the tomb opens up with a shout, that Bacchus though dead is arisen, the god is arisen, the god is alive, he was limp, he is potent.

[The Prince:] A god has his home in the heavens; but we on the earth are humanity; *how* can you wander amongst us?

[Bacchus:] Your Bacchus was born of a god and a woman; two *na*tures are fused in his being; my mother demented with love in her heart, and desire in her flesh for divinity, prayed for the potency, prayed for the power to fill her; and so it was done, she was bride to a firestorm, consumed by his ardour, her womb was ablaze with the manhood of god.

[The Prince:] How *then* could she *bear* you?

[Bacchus:] They *say*, the divinity snatched up the youngster, myself, and implaced him to grow in his thigh for gestation, to grow in his thigh, though whether the right or the left or the middle, is moot.

[The Prince:] Are you one, are you many, Year-spirit?

[Bacchus:] Not many, but one, and yet I can *be* in more places than one at a time; I am here and am there, I am *not* in the clods and the lumps, but the drops of all moisture, the dew of the grape when fermented, the milk in the breast

when a woman has borne, the water that bursts from the
rock when the rite is orgastic; I *am* and I *was* and will *be*;
in the daytime, the night-time, arousing the women to love,
to desire every shape, every substance.

[The Prince:] What *things* do they *do* in your orgy? is
woman with woman, or woman with beast, or woman with
green thing a-growing, or woman with mineral stone?

[Bacchus:] You can see for yourself, come amongst us, to
see how they eat of the god to be filled with his mana.

*[Bacchus still dancing chants solemnly — lightly touching
himself (though not his loins) with the pinecone on the
fennel stalk, at the close of the chant:]* Bacchus begotten
and born, nursed at the bosom and fondled, made love to,
the god or the beast his familiar, then savaged and eaten,
then Bacchus reborn; *[more quietly but crescendo]* how *is*
he begotten? a woman is one with the wild; and *how* is
he born? of the womb of the commune; and *nursed* through
his kindred? her nipple to serpent or fawn, with devotion,
and *that* is the moment you *can*not return from; how
*fond*led, made love to, how *sav*aged? they *fond*le without
and within, they caress him without and within, the god is
within them, the god or the beast his familiar within them;
they savage and eat him, devour him, the god or the beast
his familiar, his kindred, and one of the beasts is a man.
*[This chant is not repeated; Bacchus now touches the
Prince in the same way as he had touched himself, and
lyrically sings 'the lynx', which will be repeated, by the
women, with change of pronouns:]* The lynx is like barley

with cream, the ape and the roebuck are anise and melon, the *cham*ois like cinnamon thyme; the flesh of a child, of a manchild, a man you have borne to the god for a feast, you are *one* with his *be*ing, the flesh of a man is like snow filled with honey, snow filled with honey, the flesh of a man is like snow filled with honey.

Your Bacchus is wine of mirage and delusion, his eyes have the taste of the raisin at autumn, his fingers and toes are like figs in a syrup, the stomach as chewy as chestnuts, the heart is like pears in their luscious new-fallen red-yellow, the parts he conceals as his godhead *[here touching the loins]* the *pome*granate sugared in *cane* sweet, the *pome*granate sugared in *cane* sweet, his godhead is *cane* sweet.

[Bacchus continuing:]   Your Bacchus is wine of delusion, the flesh of a man is like snow filled with honey, like snow filled with honey *[gesture]*:   the food you consume to commune is within you; the god will reply and be merry, the god will reply by dispersing his mana, dispelling the seed of his loins into fruit; every stigma or style of a pistil, or stalk of a stamen, is filled with desire — all gonads are heavy and glad in his worship, all vesicles filled with a serum of joy.

The world will be fertile and frolic with Bacchus, the dew and the pulse of his mana; the sheep will conceive now, the wheat will be grainy, the olive be plump with a goodness, the butterfly strew all the meadow with daisies; your god will return by and by, or his likeness, reborn as another, another be yours for caressing and suckling, and yours for the womb intromission, *[repeating]* and yours for the womb intromission, and yours for the mouth to devour.

[Bacchus now says (having found a razor to shear the Prince, and giving him the pinecone rod):] I must dress you to pass as a woman, your beard must be shorn to the blood, with a dusting of milkweed, the skin of a woman; your sandals, your belt with its dagger — we trade for bare feet and a cord at the bosom, a sign of exchanging in gender, and the emblem of god, the pinecone erect on the stalk, you must brandish; the costume will make you immune to their hunger, the women will think you are one of their number; a man that they found would be game, would be prey, they might *do* what the urging within them desired; and besides when you dress as a woman, *that* is a moment of magic, you *are* then a woman becoming, your eyes flirt with love, and your thoughts and your wants are a woman's. *[Bacchus takes back the pinecone rod and touches the Prince with it and then returns it to him.]*

[The Prince, touching himself:] I sense a contraction with wrinkling and swelling, my parts are their counterparts, male into female, and *will* into *will*ing, my will is transformed into willing, my parts that were male are transformed inside out into female; no, rather my elements mingle together as lovers, a man and a woman in union; no, rather the parts have remained as they were but respond to desire as their counterparts would, I am *male* but my senses are female.

[Bacchus:] Dear fellow, myself in another, now trust me, and *I* will be *with* you and *that* will be all the safeguarding you need, me *with* you when ravenous women want god as a man in their body and eat him to know of the sweetness.

[The women, now with the pinecone rod and with leaves in their hair, enter the orchestra dancing, and sing — one by one, not in unison — the first stanza of 'the lynx':] The lynx is like barley with cream, the ape and the roebuck are anise and melon, the *cham*ois like cinnamon thyme; the flesh of a child, of a manchild, a man we have borne to the god for a feast, we are *one* with his *be*ing, the flesh of a man is like snow filled with honey, snow filled with honey, the flesh of a man is like snow filled with honey.

[The women now see Bacchus (in his yellow dress) and the Prince (in homespun); the Prince has the pinecone rod, Bacchus does not; they are alike in manner, but differ greatly in physical type; the women say:] They took him away, we have found him two*fold*, our vision is double, a sign of dementia, or *is* it the god and a sister, the body of man in a woman, the senses of woman in man? They took him away, we have found him. *[The women sing, one by one, the whole of 'the lynx' lyrically:]* The lynx is like barley with cream, the ape and the roebuck are anise and melon, the chamois like cinnamon thyme; the flesh of a child, of a manchild, a man we have borne to the god for a feast, we are *one* with his *be*ing, the flesh of a man is like snow filled with honey, snow filled with honey, the flesh of a man is like snow filled with honey.

Our Bacchus is wine of mirage and delusion, his eyes have the taste of the raisin at autumn, his fingers and toes are like figs in a syrup, the stomach as chewy as chestnuts, the heart is like pears in their luscious new-fallen red-yellow, the parts he conceals as his godhead *[here touching the loins]* the *pome*granate sugared in *cane* sweet, the *pome*granate sugared in *cane* sweet, his godhead is *cane* sweet.

Our Bacchus is wine of delusion, the flesh of a man is like snow filled with honey, like snow filled with honey *[gesture]*: the food you consume to commune is within you; the god will reply and be merry, the god will reply by dispersing his mana, dispelling the seed of his loins into fruit; every stigma or style of a pistil, or stalk of a stamen, is filled with desire, — all gonads are heavy and glad in his worship, all vesicles filled with a serum of joy.

The world will be fertile and frolic with Bacchus, the dew and the pulse of his mana; the sheep will conceive now, the wheat will be grainy, the olive be plump with a goodness, the butterfly strew all the meadow with daisies; your god will return by and by, or his likeness, reborn as another, another be yours for caressing and suckling, and yours for the womb intromission, *[repeating]* and yours for the womb intromission, and yours for the mouth to devour.

[The women (with one hand, while the other brandishes the rod) caress and fondle each other on the cheek, the bosom, and the loins (and, if it can be managed, the same with snakes, lynxes, and such, with suckling and intro-mission), at some length; drums, clarinets, faint when the women sing, louder when they do not; the women come to Bacchus and the Prince on stage; Bacchus takes the rod and, brandishing it, dances away from the Prince; half of the women follow him; the other half (with their free hand) caress and fondle the Prince delicately on his cheek, and say:] I am sensing the sun in eclipse and the rocks in an earthquake, the heavens in thunder, the god is caressing my body, is fondling my secret desires. *[Now the women touch the Prince at his bosom and loins, and say:]* Is the body

of man in a woman, or body of woman in man? *[They touch him, though it is only to be surmised whether they discover that he is a man (or that he has become a woman); the stage is filled with mist; drums, for eclipse earthquake thunder. The Prince has presumably been torn and eaten, for —]*

[All the women (surprise) come through the mist into the orchestra from byways, without the pinecone rod, eating from food in their hands; they say:] My pet and my lover, the god I commune with, I suckle the god, intromit him, I eat of my god, of my Bacchus, I eat of his likeness, his kindred. *[The women now sing, one by one, the first two stanzas of 'the lynx':]* The lynx is like barley with cream, the ape and the roebuck are anise and melon, the chamois like cinnamon thyme; the flesh of a child, of a manchild, a man we have borne to the god for a feast, we are *one* with his *bei*ng, the flesh of a man is like snow filled with honey, snow filled with honey, the flesh of a man is like snow filled with honey.

Our Bacchus is wine of mirage and delusion, his eyes have the taste of the raisin at autumn, his fingers and toes are like figs in a syrup, the stomach as chewy as chestnuts, the heart is like pears in their luscious new-fallen red-yellow, the parts he conceals as his godhead *[here touching the loins]* the *pome*granate sugared in *cane* sweet, the *pome*granate sugared in *cane* sweet, his godhead is *cane* sweet. *[The women gorge themselves senseless; drums, clarinets; the music fades; the women recover with tears, beating their breasts, and say quietly, one by one:]* These gobbets are *meat*, they are *not* like the snow filled with honey, nor barley with cream, nor pears in their luscious red-yellow; our hands and our faces are crimson with *meat* blood, are scarlet and crimson with *meat*; not the snow filled with honey nor barley with cream, but the scarlet and crimson of *meat*; if a lynx or a roebuck or chamois, then *where* is the *fur*, where the *hide* of that creature? or *was* it a wandering *man* on the mountain, some *man* pulled apart in our frenzy of hunger and lust? have we eaten the eyes and the toes and the manhood of someone a woman had borne from her womb? what demon, what goblin, impelled us, what war-lock or witch? are we mothers who ate of a child, from desire to be one with the god, are the scarlet and crimson the blood of a child, did we eat of a child, of a man, from an urge to have Bacchus within us? Remorse now forever, remorse in the afterworld, wakeful, no longer in dreams of delusion, but eating a manchild, his eyes and his toes and the loins of his manhood, the loins of his manhood, awake and aware; what horror of madness implanted the hunger, the itch of desire in our nipple, our womb and our mouth, the desire to devour all his parts in our mouth?

[Now all seems to be over; but the Prince, from a byway, the music preceding him as it did Bacchus before, appears in the yellow garb of Bacchus with the lynx skin and the . letter B, and brandishes the pinecone rod, — as if he had taken the place of the god; touches the women with the cone, solemnly chants with dancing:] Women, take Bacchus wit*hin* you; women, take *god* to your body;

women, old women, young women, half women — women, take *god* to your body, and give of your body to *god*. Women with milk, leave your sucklings at home, you may suckle the god, give your milk to the *god*, your breast in the mouth of his kindred, your nipple to fawn or to serpent.

The stalk of the fennel, the cone of the pine, the emblem of Bacchus, of man in his manhood, of man and of bull and of stallion and ram, of a man in the strength of the girth of his loins, when his energy flows from his mind and his heart to his loins, like a torrent in springtime, when conscience is vassal, desire suzer*ain*; I will teach you to brandish the stalk of the fennel, the cone of the pine.

Blessèd is time in destruction, blessèd is time when renewed, as the *year* comes around in a wheel, nor is time like an arrow, not forward nor backward but round and around, for destruction renewal destruction; the wild is a claw and a fang to the tame, you are leaving your houses and temples, your homes are the mountain, your altars the forest, your *con*jury north of the north wind.

Women, take god in your innards, take god with devotion, pay homage, dismember the god and devour him, the god whom you suckled, your nipple to serpent or fawn; now devour him, his flesh and his heart and his loins, you are *one* with the god, he with *you*; come, be *mine*, come, be *one* with your Bacchus, devour him, be *one* with your god, come to suckle, dismember, devour. *[The women follow him as they had followed Bacchus, along the byway or through the nave of the theatre, with music and revelry.]*

Overview and Synopses, *The Duel, Odu*

A modern audience may be familiar, as an ancient one would have been, with many of the personae in these two plays, from the Homeric poems. (In *The Duel*, Helen and Paris from *The Iliad* 6.313-358, Dromaki and Hector from 6.369-502, and the others from 9.663-668; in *Odu*, Clip from *The Odyssey* 5.14, Now from 6.17, Circe from 10.135, Penny from 23.10, Thane from 1.44, and Clay from 11.85.) But the plays go their own way. In *The Duel*, Paris may be a god, and Helen a phantom; the happenings are reversed, as if all were being done and then for some reason undone; and the locale is not what we thought it was. In *Odu*, the women are a multiple role: they resemble each other, and there is reason why they should do. For both plays the mise-en-scène is a level area before a mound.

Characters and garments, *The Duel*: four females, four males, all of the same age: *f m*, speaking, active, Helen and Paris; *f f*, speaking, less active, Dromaki (*Draw*makee) and If; *m m*, not speaking, active, Hector and Patrock (Pa*trawk*); *f m*, not speaking, less active, Midi (*Mee*dee) and Akill (Ah-*kill*). The Trojans (Paris, Dromaki, Hector) may be of a different racial type from the Greeks (Helen, Patrock, Akill); If and Midi, captives from islands, resemble the Trojans. All are lightly clothed in tunics with a cord at the waist and without undergarments. When the play is performed with *The Women* (where the beard is a sign of masculinity), the men are bearded, perhaps not heavily.

Characters and garments, *Odu*: one male, *O*du; one female as Clip, Now, Circe (*Sir*see), Penny, Thane, Clay. He and they are of the same racial type, for one of the women is his mother. Clothing as in *The Duel*.

Setting and properties, *The Duel*: male-female and female-male pairs on the left, Paris-and-Helen, Dromaki-and-Hector; similarly on the right, Patrock-and-If, Midi-and-Akill; If and Midi each have a hand on the other's breast. All are half reclining, with fleeces as pillows, against a mound (shaped like a breast, though not conspicuously so); and in such a posture they remain throughout, except that: Helen dances or tumbles from place to place, and the men are upright during the duel. At hand are: a bow, two golden arrows, and gloves for Paris; the spear of Akill; large nondescript skins of water, sponges, small red skins for blood, small spangled skins for myrrh; and willow withes.

Setting and properties, *Odu*: Odu and the women are upright throughout. The mound is in the background. There are no properties; the wand of Circe is spoken of but not seen. If the performance is indoors, the mound may be lighted gradually in the last two scenes, for it is then a memorial to the breast of Clay, which Odu caresses.

Synopsis of *The Duel*: About the Trojan War. Two heroes are armed; they fight each other; there is an aftermath.

Opening: a sponging with water from a waterskin, words, caresses, a tasting by all of the blood from a bloodskin: one event after another:

a) Helen rouses Paris, they sponge each other, speak to each other, and put a skin of blood to each other's lips

b) Helen arcs to Midi and If, takes the hand of each from the other's breast, and rouses Midi

c) Paris rouses Dromaki

d) Helen rouses If and arcs back

e) Dromaki rouses Hector and arms him

f) If rouses Patrock and arms him, speaking; at the same time Midi rouses Akill, not speaking

Middle: combat: sumo-style, slow motion, balletic; sound of sword on shield; Hector and Patrock wrestle; Paris, with an arrow in each hand, and Akill, with his spear, are their seconds; Paris stabs Patrock in the belly with the lefthand arrow; Akill wounds Hector with his spear; Paris shatters the spear with his lefthand arrow, and then stabs Akill in the heel with the righthand arrow; whether the injured will recover is uncertain

Closing: a sponging with water from a waterskin, words, caresses, a tasting by all of the myrrh from a myrrhskin: one event after another; an exact reversal:

f] If disarms and grieves over Patrock, speaking; at the same time Midi grieves over Akill, not speaking

e] Dromaki disarms and grieves over Hector

d] Helen arcs to If and Midi, and comforts If

c] Paris comforts Dromaki

b] Helen comforts Midi, puts a hand of Midi and If on the other's breast, and arcs back

a] Helen quiets Paris, they sponge each other, speak to each other, and put a skin of myrrh to the other's lips

Synopsis of *Odu*: Odu speaks about his women — those he encountered on his return (Clip, Now, Circe, Penny) and those who are his inborn idea of woman (Thane, Clay). The women appear one by one, the same in looks but different in manner.

Hector and Patrock

The Duel

a): *[Helen wakes, sits up, pours water onto sponges, and sponges her face, singing or speaking with melody:]* Wash away sleep from the eyelids, sponge off the grime and the sorrows of yesterday. Gone are the stars of the bear and the hunter. Gone is the fragrance of balm for the wounds of the mind and the body, the myrrh like a cobbler who stitches in darkness, the Nubian resin benumbing their anguish, the anodyne drug of the healer. The bitter, the sweet of the feast are forgotten; the scavenger ants in the night have consumed the remains. Green tendrils have grown, and the brown slough *[sluff]* away. It is time to rehearse the enactment.

[Helen now speaking, to no one in particular, with a gesture indicating those across the way:] The rhombus of lovers, the lesbian loving of Midi and If, the dorian love of Akill and Patrock, with the hetero loves of Akill and his Midi, Patrock and his If. She dreams of *her,* he of *him,* but *then* they embrace their bed*fel*lows asleep, she with *him,* he with *her,* they are *one,* and their thoughts become one with their bodies. So Midi makes love to Akill and to If, and If to Patrock and to Midi.

[Helen to Paris, sponging his face and then fondling him:] Paris the godlike for beauty of manhood, Apollo himself in the hide of a panther *[only words: there is no hide]*, weaponed with arrows of gold, belovèd by women whose love is for men, belovèd as well by the men who love comrades. Looming and fading as prince or as god, you appear in their dream and their daydream. I *think* it is Paris my darling I touch, but is it Apollo, forsaking

Olympus, forsaking his arrows the sunbeams? Apollo or Paris, *[Helen putting the red skin to his lips:]* freshen your lips with the blood that emboldens our heart to do mayhem.

[Paris taking the red skin from Helen, putting it aside, fondling her:] Helen belovèd by men who love women, belovèd as well by the women whose love is for women, all men and all women in love with a woman make love to a dream or a daydream and say to themselves they are lovers of Helen. Skeleton key into wedlock, how many the faithful or faithless whose thoughts unconfess'd are desiring the touches of Helen? How many the men and the women who *shut* out the world with their eyes and embrace you? *[Putting the red skin to her mouth:]* Your lips taste the blood that brings death into life, as the wages of all who do harm.

[Helen to Paris:] You appear in a dream as Akill to Patrock and to Midi, to If and Akill as Patrock; you are Hector to Dromaki. My Paris-Apollo, majestic in *con*tour, belovèd for art in the craft, they say you are god among lovers. Your Helen was willing to love Menelaus her husband, but then she saw you.

[Paris to Helen:] You are If in a dream to Patrock and to Midi, and Midi to If and Akill; and to Hector his Dromaki. Shape and response, in form and in motion, they say that my Helen is alpha omega. In dreams Menelaus your husband embraces your body, refusing all others awake as he longs for a visit from you in his sleep.

[Helen:] I will *rouse* up the lesbian Midi and If, but let *them* awaken the dorian comrades Akill and Patrock, their loves in a rhombus.

[Paris:] And *I* will rouse Hector and Dromaki, wholly devoted forever as halves uncombining with others, though Helen and Paris may come to embrace them as phantoms.

b): *[Helen moves from Paris to Midi, in an arc between the audience and Dromaki-and-Hector; then:]* It is day, darling Midi, leave Lesbos behind, the isle of your child-hood, the rocks and the sands and the mollusc whose dye is the bluest of purple, where women return the affection of women. Leave If with your thoughts and your hands *[Helen takes the hands of Midi and If from the other's breast]*. In a dream you were touching her body, with notions of touching yourself only sweeter, and *she* dreamt the same about you. Darling Midi, come rouse up Akill, to give strength to his comrade Patrock, with the myrmidon spear ithyphallic, the sign of his clan. Akill is immune, do not *fear* for him. Helen your friend who adores you speaks truly. *[With sponge and the red skin:]* Taste of the blood-skin.

c): *[Paris to Dromaki who, now that Helen has left, is lying almost beside him:]* Dromaki wife of dour Hector my brother the main man of Troy, I would enter your dream in his likeness *[caresses her]*. Wake slowly and gently, *[with a sponge and with the skin to her lips:]* and rouse up your husband for combat with longbone Patrock. Today is the day of the duel; forgotten the aches and the wounds of old yesterdays. Hector sleeps sound, wake him up, and prepare him for war. I will guard him with arrows. Your Paris is fond of you both, and I know from your tears of your anguish.

d): *[Helen to If:]* Darling If come ashore, come awake from your Scyrus the island of bones, the isle of the relics of heroes, the home of old femurs and jaws. Darling If, now the Hector of Troy is upon you. Awaken Patrock, your belovèd of men, though for Midi your love is not less. Give him courage and bind up his loins from assault. For I see in your tears of your anguish; I *will* not betray you. *[Sponge and bloodskin. Helen returns to her earlier position, and she and Paris touch each other, out of the action, until he takes part in the duel.]*

e): *[Dromaki to Hector:]* Other part of me Hector, wake *up* and drink courage *[sponge and bloodskin]*. Put *on* the grim bracelet of enemy kidneys and thumbs, as trophies of menace *[only words: there is no bracelet]*. Your ribcage can fend and your eyes can look *after* themselves, *[begins to wrap withes around his ankles]* but your feet and your ankles need withes of the willow. A word that is bruited about, from Apollo or Paris your brother, makes tell of a warrior greater than others — who else than yourself? — that was dipped in the river of death at his birth, but was held by the heel, and is not to be scathed except there, where the stream did not touch him. *[She begins to wrap withes round about his loins, beneath the tunic, but without lewdness or a showing of nakedness:]* Your stones as the heirlooms of Troy, all the wealth of the city forever, pull

*in*to your body, against the raw thrust of a mauler or clout.
Your manliness hide in your innards, my Hector, my darling
and strength, other part of myself. Make war with the care
and the muscle you give me in loving.

  [Dromaki to Hector, continuing:] Akill with his myrmidon spear ithyphallic would shatter the rules of the combat, but Paris-Apollo your brother holds watch with his
arrows, those arrows that strike at my womb in a dream of
pollution, and *in*to my daydreams invade like the army of
vermin I sweep out of doors, to keep the house tidy for *you*,
my good husband. For no-one but *you* knows me
wholly, and *you* are within every pore, every sinus, and *I*
will be *with* you, my heartbeat in yours, di*a*stolë *sy*stolë
thumping in time with each other, now *I* am in*side* you,
completing you, making you whole, as you are to me.

f): *[If to Patrock:]* Bed*fe*llow Patrock my belovèd, wake
up and give mouth to raw fortitude *[sponge and bloodskin]*.
Wear now the necklace of livers and tongues you have cut
from the Trojans, to warn them take heed *[only words:
there is no necklace]*. Let me bind the pale withes
[wrapping them about his ankles], with the thorn of
acanthus *[only words: there is no acanthus]*, to strengthen
your ankles. A prophecy tells that Patrock or Akill,
yourself or yourself-in-another, will suffer as*trag*alus harm,
the tendon undipped in the Styx. *[Now the withes about
his loins, but without lewdness or display:]* And your
foreskin adorned with tattoos of the emblem of cunning,
wrap well for your *bed*fellow If and your comrade Akill.
Your manliness matters to us; I believe that it matters the
most.

[Midi rouses Akill, not speaking; If continues, to Patrock:] The Hector is bloody in thought for revenge, but my fear is the arrow of Paris his brother in league with Apollo. Against them, my darling Patrock, and Akill with the myrmidon spear ithyphallic. For *he* is within you; his knee bends with yours and his arm within yours makes a blow; your hearts are in time, the toughest of hearts and the grandest. The knowledge you have of his body, and he has of yours, that knowledge will double your strength.

Combat sumo-style, in slow motion, balletic, with background sound of sword on shield; no words but possibly grunts and groans. Hector and Patrock wrestle; Paris, wearing gloves and holding an arrow in each hand, moves about them from side to side; Akill with his spear stands firm; Paris stabs Patrock in the belly with the lefthand arrow; Akill wounds Hector with his spear; Paris shatters the spear with his lefthand arrow, and then stabs Akill in the heel with the righthand arrow. The weapons are withdrawn straightway; whether the injured will recover is uncertain.

f]: *[As Midi grieves over Akill, not speaking, If grieves over Patrock, speaking:]* My longbone Patrock, Akill and his body and myrmidon spear ithyphallic were slow to protect you. Unequal to Paris-Apollo whose arrows would shatter a rampart. *[Unbinding the withes from his loins, without a display of nakedness:]* Tattered the foreskin with emblems and shrivelled the manliness. *[Unbinding the ankles:]* Useless the binding of heel with the withes and the thorn of acanthus. Undaunting the garland of livers and tongues you had shorn from the Trojans. Belovèd bed*fe*llow Patrock, *[sponge and myrrhskin, and so for Midi to Akill; If continues:]* wash *clean* of the battle and drink up the anodyne myrrh for embalming to sleep as I suffer.

e]: *[Dromaki grieving over Hector:]* My Hector, the care and affection, the heartbeat in time with your own, unavailing. Akill and his myrmidon tore through your innards. *[Unbinding the withes, without a display of nakedness:]* The stones that were heirlooms of Troy are as lumps of red clay and the city is sterile. The withes of the willow, the bracelet of kidneys and thumbs, unavailing. My life unavailing, the worth of my body; *[sponge and myrrhskin]* I will wash you and give you to sup of the myrrh.

d]: *[Helen arcs to If, speaks:]* Darling If, I can tell of your pain as you loosen the withes from the loins of Patrock your belovèd. *[Takes the sponge and myrrhskin from her, wipes her eyes, gives her to taste:]* Wipe your eyes, taste the drug, sail away to your Scyrus, the island of bones, go to sleep till tomorrow, to sleep till I wake you.

c]: *[Paris to Dromaki:]* Lovely Dromaki, anguish I see in the tears of your eyelids in tending the body of Hector. Now sleep till the time comes, *[sponge and myrrhskin]* to sleep and to dream in the dark and to heal from the light with its agony.

b]: *[Helen to Midi:]* Midi my darling *[sponge and myrrhskin]*, embrace in a dream gaunt Akill, and leave for a moment the kingdom of pain. *[Puts a hand of Midi and If on the other's breast:]* Sail to Lesbos the isle of the rocks and the sands and the mollusc, the isle of affection. *[Helen arcs back.]*

a]: *[Paris to Helen:]* Now Hector is sleeping and Dromaki, wholly devoted as halves of each other, regaining their health in the trance of the drug.

[Helen to Paris:] And asleep are the loves in a rhombus, the dorian comrades Patrock and Akill with the lesbian If and her Midi, a man by a woman.

[Paris:] My Helen will wander among them, as If or as Midi, or Dromaki, alpha omega my Helen for shape and response, in form and in motion, to gladden their dreams.

[Helen:] Becoming Patrock or Akill, or the Hector, my Paris-Apollo will wander among them as well, whose *contour* and art in the craft make him god among lovers.

[Paris fondling Helen, putting the sponge to her face, the myrrhskin to her lips:] Taste of the solace and slumber, and walk into byways of thought unconfess'd, of the men and the women who say to themselves they are lovers of Helen.

[Helen putting the sponge and the myrrhskin to him:] Slumber yourself, then arise and with arrows of gold like Apollo come *in*to the dreams of the women whose love is for men and the dreams of the men who love comrades.

[Continuing, now to no-one in particular, as if musing to herself:] What will the day be tomorrow for If and her Midi, Patrock and Akill, for Hector and Dromaki? Arming tomorrow again, and a duel, and anguish. As life in the afterlife, here where we are, in the afterlife, everywhere, nowhere. An afterlife duel of honour, disrupted by treachery, muscle impaired by a spear or an arrow. An afterlife duel of men and a torment for women. Tomorrow, an underworld day like another, an afterlife moment recurring forever, a book without end, a book of identical chapters. The thought that they died with, the sum of their lifetime on earth, enduring forever, last thoughts enduring forever, an underworld afterlife moment forever. Enacted once more the performance. All has been done and undone for redoing tomorrow forever. My Paris-Apollo and I will be kind to them.

[With melody as at the beginning:] Tendrils are drooping, scavenger ants are consuming their feast, the Nubian fragrance of resin is numbing my senses, the stars of the bear and the hunter return.

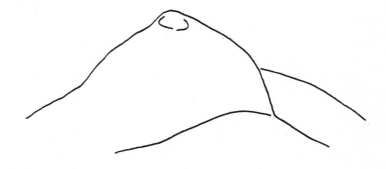

The Mound of *The Duel* and *Odu*

Odu

a): *[Odu speaking as in Iliad 3.217-223: 'He would lean
on his staff and look down at the ground, and you would
think him an oaf; but when the voice came from his chest,
and the words fell like snow, then no-one could compare
with him':]* My way homewards had come to the cave of
the succubus Clip, whose freckles would fracture the heart
with their beauty, the earthy but heavenly Clip; and I
entered her mansion through passages lost of return, to the
dens of her grotto. She bathed me in spray from a whirlpool and scraped off the scurf, anointed my bruises with
unguents made fragrant by cypress, and clothed me in garments as soft as the wool of the beaver — tunics with
blasphemous emblems, mantles deep-dyed by the shellfish
of Proteus, bluehaired old man of the sea who on land is
lord Bacchus, lord Bacchus the god we resemble whenever
desire is upon us. And *gave* me to eat of her savoury harvest, and spoke with a whisper, and led me to intricate
hinges and levers and wheels, contrivances wrought for the
making of love. And drained with the clamp of her womb
my virility, hour after hour, day, month after month, as a
vampire whose fang is a pleasure the gods would create for
themselves.

b): *[Clip enters, coaxing him with gestures, brushing
against him, kissing him quickly here and there, offering
fruit:]* Darling Odu, these kumquats and papaws
besprinkled with dawnleaf are luscious, tasting to me like
yourself, filling my veins with desire; they are firm as if
ripe at the moment, take bites with your lips on their labia,

see if their texture reminds you of me, will they tremble and yield at your touch? The machines and contraptions enhancing our coming together are ready, have joy in me, bring me to joy, O my Odu, my darling, my Bacchus, the part of your Clip that was missing *[she leaves].*

c):   *[Odu resumes:]* Pulling myself from her body, the cave of my sojourn, I trudged a path homewards again, when a cyclone made fun with me, smashing me, stripping me bare as a newborn, hurling me dead in a ditch, where I slept, and awoke with exhaustion, and slept, until after a night and a morning the power returned to my shoulders and midriff and tools. When a bundle of goodness named Now, in a game with her handmaids, found me a satyr asleep. I was dreaming of nymphs and of goats and the way I might enter their bodies, when Now halfway smiling, with dimples a demon would honour, enrobed my indecency, covered my muscular masculine shame of desire with the cloth from her picnic. I woke like a warrior whose weapon is stark through his armour.

d):   *[Now enters, girlish:]* Finders keepers, I claim you, a stranger blown *into* this village where all of us know all the others too well. My blushes have told you I saw you complete in your manhood, your strength makes me weaken, a man that a girl would be happy to have and to hold, they say it is time for betrothal, to gather the flowers of spring. Come along to my house, meet my parents and brothers, the house of my parents, time I should manage a house of my own, try your arm on my brothers in wrestling, I think they will find you their equal *[she leaves].*

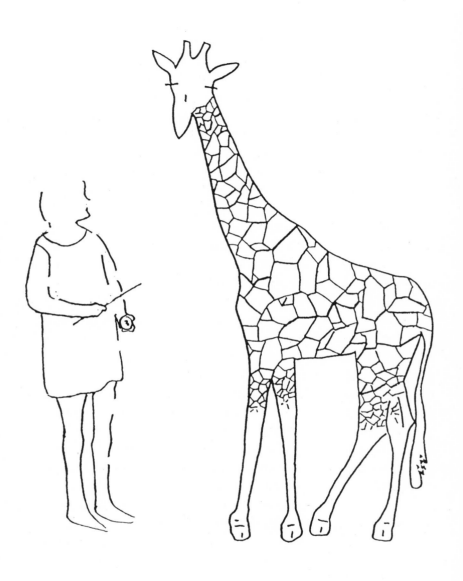

Circe and a Companion

e): *[Odu:]* I left her a peach for the plucking, and came to a garden of rhinos and zebras, of hippo, giraffe and hyena, playful and tame, constrictors in knots from their intricate sporting together, pets of a keeper named Circe. They bounded around her, greeting her friendly but longing for something; I thought, Were they men? are they men she enchanted? I saw for a moment her wand; did the beasts have a witch for their warden? I lingered amused by the counterfeit pouts and the winks of her lashes, the turns and the hollows, the ins and the outs of that country the body of Circe, a landscape of peril. She finished my sentences, gestured which way I should go, where to sit, when to hum; and clothed me in down of disdain from her swans, and in filaments stolen from spiders, cocoons that cecropia moths at their leisure had wound from the gems on their leathery wings; I was fettered, enchanted.

f): *[Circe enters without wand, pets him, gestures magically with her hands, and acts like her animals as she mentions them:]* Odu my pet, are the elephants most to your liking, or is it the calico tigers, who purr and rub with affection? or the bears as they offer their paws full of honey? Join in the mischief with sunfish that bathe in the midst of the midday, or ravens that think they make sense when they speak, with the rabbits that wrinkle their noses and listen intently, or squirrels that bury brown walnuts for hardships a-coming. My pet, darling Odu, my pet and my darling, stay *with* me, stay *here* as my pet, I will care for you *[she leaves]*.

g): *[Odu:]* I got home to the meaningless laughter of
Penny, she bathed me and clothed me in gorgeous apparel,
a tunic and robe of her weaving. And *that* was the moment
I knew that the others who also had clothed me, had covered me naked, were shadows, adventures; the succubus
Clip (whose freckles had fractured my heart with their
beauty) and Now (who had smiled with the dimples a
demon would honour) and Circe (bewitching with lashes
and winks): all had brought me to Penny. I knew then the
pastimes were past, for the freckles that once had detained
me, the dimples, the lashes, were hers; the women I found
by the wayside were she in their wrists and their ankles, the
flats and fossettes of their belly, the flaws in their
symmetry, manner and gesture. In loving them all I was
faithful to her.

h): *[Penny enters, vague, laughing:]* They *told* me that
Odu was dead, I should marry another. I said, let me
weave for my bridegroom a robe bearing signs of good
luck on its fringe and a symbol. I wove, but the signs and
the symbol would not come out right, I wove and I ravelled
and wove; the robe was a time in the making. At last it
was done; then you came, and they fled; they fled when
you came, so I *thought* it was you. I should not have been
sure, for one *man* is to *me* all the same as another, one
beard or one biceps or basso, one ocean or star or one
sheep or one wine or one table or plough, all the same.
Then a thing that I knew came within me; I said to myself
it was *you*, for not knowing another I thought your append-
age unique; be honest, are men all alike in that quarter, are
others the same as yourself? *[she leaves]*.

i): *[Odu:]* From my earliest days I have worshipped a goddess, my thane or companion, the form of a woman, or pattern, invoked her in dreams and in daydreams, conjured her out from my innards with *am*brota*tha*na, the mystical sentences *ambrotathana maranatha, ambrotathana, ambrotathana maranatha.* Thane theanthropic, memory sown with his seed by my father, inherent instinctive folk wisdom begotten within me, a will-o'-the-wisp whom I beckon, or serve as a serf. And she never tells what I should *do* but will often forbid what my rashness has led to; I left the old Nestor to fight for himself, and he *called* me pol*troon*; it was Thane who had said to escape or die *with* him. My thane in the form of a woman is Penny; Thane *gave* me her, *her* and her likeness in Clip and in Now and in Circe. Most truly my goddess and helpmeet is Thane, my idea of a woman, companion in dreams and in daydreams, nor could I in daydream or dream of my thane ever touch her, no more than myself.

j): *[Thane enters, austere, distant, with the appropriate gestures of measurement:]* Do you love me, dear Odu? your goddess and servant begotten within, your companion and thane, folk wisdom inherent instinctive. The lore that you need I have given, the form of a woman, the pattern: the truncated cones in her upper and forearms, her thighs and her calves; parallelepipeds her hands; each buttock a pyramid frustum; the body a work of geometry anthropometric. The length of a head from the chin to the line of the nipples, a head from the line of the nips to the button, three heads from the pit of the arm to the end of the finger, proportions a marvel of nature. The curve of her eye is the same as the curve of the groin from the iliac spine to the pubis. And so you love Penny. Lord Bacchus is summoned whenever the conjuror handles the magical runes in the pyramid frusta, the curve of the groin from the iliac spine, or the teardrops that swell from her thorax; and Bacchus has brought you together *[she leaves]*.

k): *[Odu:]* My thane — my companion, my inner idea of a woman, bequeathed and begotten by ancestors ancient as time — was friends with my father as well. So my Thane is the image and wraith of my mother, called Clay. Here is proof I am son to my father, as sure as my curl or my timbre; the notion of woman in *him* is the same as the notion with*in* me, the image of Clay; he sowed me as seed and implanted the image. So *she* whom I took in betrothal was thought like her sister, her sister or daughter, no stranger, no daughter-in-law unrelated by bloodlines. Physicians examining Penny for marriage, the dressmaker measuring bodice and lilt, found Penny and Clay to be peas of a pod. The women I knew by the wayside were Penny and Thane and were *Clay*; it was Clay I would stay with sojourning, and *she* whom I longed to return to, *she* was the pattern, my inner idea. The magical runes I would handle in woman, invoking lord Bacchus, belonged at the last to my mother. *I* was the fruit of her womb, and for *her* was the fruit of my loins; the Bacchus that surged in my body was wanting my mother, my Clay, who should afterwards *be* my companion and Thane, and my Penny, and those whom I knew by the wayside.

l): *[Clay enters, grave but warm:]* Do you love my breasts or the breasts of the woman who nursed you? Your

father would have me remain as I was at our wedding, for
him and for you: for him as a body desired, and for you as
a model of what you should find in another, to love and to
lie with. The mind he begot in yourself has my likeness as
imprint and birthright, and *you* call her Thane. That likeness I *was* to preserve, both the shape and the style, for the
sake of your *see*ing the pattern in*born* in the flesh of your
mother. To *keep* the beauty about me, I gave you away to
be suckled; your love is divided between us, the wet nurse
and me. But the image provoking desire, the runes of lord
Bacchus, *these* I have kept to be *with* you all day from your
childhood. A man can make love to his mother, and a
woman to son, if her breasts are still lovely, I know of an
instance; but who would make love to the nourishing pen-
dulous uberous breasts of a nurse, her teats chewed and
ragged? *[leaves]*.

m): *[Odu:]* Beautiful Clay is as dead as her name. They
say it was longing for me, or in longing for *him*, the green
yeoman my father had been, as my mother desired us, and
wanting us, one in the other, grew lonely and died. And
then he as well, the sands of the seasons allotted had run
through the glass. The bones of my parents are mingled
together. But *in* his last moment of life he planned a
memorial mound to my mother, a mound made in clay, for
the name of the Clay he had loved, with the shape of her
beautiful breast; and this is my woman, my Clay and my
Thane and my Penny, my Circe and Now and my Clip, the
runestone invoking lord Bacchus, my Clay and my Thane
and my Penny, my Clay and my love *[caresses the breast,
finally the nipple]*.

DATE DUE

MAY 21 '07		